Southern Living

Low-Fat
Low-Calorie
RECIPES

Southern Living

OUR BEST

Low-Fat
Low-Calorie
RECIPES

Compiled by
Jean Wickstrom Liles

Edited by
Lisa Hooper Talley

GOOD HEALTH WITH GREAT TASTE

It's a fact: You want foods that are low in fat and calories,

but you also want those foods to taste good.

page 227

With *Our Best Low-Fat, Low-Calorie Recipes*, you'll never have to compromise flavor for nutrition. Just one sample from this collection of top-rated light recipes from *Southern Living* magazine, and you'll see what we mean. These

page 106

recipes had to pass three stringent tests: They had to be low in fat, low in calories, and taste so good that we'd prepare them for our own families. These winning recipes will take you from appetizers to desserts and everywhere in between. You'll also find menus for weeknight suppers, casual gatherings, and festive dinners. From cover to cover, these pages are bursting with tempting surprises. And speaking of the cover,

page 132

we're introducing a new lightened version of our readers' all-time favorite recipe—Hummingbird Cake. Since appearing in the February 1978 issue of the magazine, it has been our most requested recipe. We've revamped this classic into a guilt-free treat just for you—Light Hummingbird Cake (page 225). Now you can have your cake and eat it too!

6

TEST YOUR NUTRITION IQ

Take this quick quiz to find out how nutrition savvy you are.

Question: **True or False?** To eat healthfully, you must gradually replace your favorite foods that are considered "bad" with nutritious "good" foods.
Answer: **False.** No single food is "good" or "bad." Instead, it's what you consume during an entire day or several days that counts. Variety, balance, and moderation are the keys to healthy eating.

Question: Snacking between meals can
    A. prevent overeating
    B. boost energy level
    C. satisfy cravings and improve mood
    D. all of the above
Answer: **D.** Skipping meals or eating erratically can lead to energy slumps, mood swings, and overeating at meals. Research shows that eating six minimeals and snacking throughout the day can help control your weight and energize your body.

Question: **True or False?** Trimming the visible fat from meat gets rid of the cholesterol.
Answer: **False.** Cholesterol is found in the meat *and* the fat. When you trim the visible fat, you reduce the cholesterol, but you don't eliminate it.

Question: When you hear, "Consume no more than 30 percent of calories from fat," what does this include?
    A. every food you eat
    B. foods consumed in one day
    C. foods consumed over several days
Answer: **C.** The 30-percent-of-calories-from-fat guideline refers to the foods consumed over several days. If you consume a food that is over 30 percent of calories from fat, it's okay. Just combine that food with low-fat foods to bring the average of that meal or meals to 30 percent or less of calories from fat.

Question: **True or False?** Foods low in fat are low in calories.
Answer: **False.** Cutting fat doesn't mean that calories are cut as well. Many low-fat and nonfat products have added sugar and contain as many calories as regular versions—and sometimes more.

Question: When nutrition experts say, "Eat five a day," what do they mean?
    A. eat one food from each of the five food groups daily
    B. eat at least five servings of fruits and vegetables daily
    C. eat three meals plus two snacks daily
Answer: **B.** Eat at least three vegetable servings and two fruit servings daily for good health. Fruits and vegetables are naturally low in fat and calories, yet high in vitamins and minerals.

Question: Which is the healthiest?
    A. margarine in tub or liquid form
    B. margarine in stick form
    C. any type of margarine
Answer: **A.** The American Heart Association recommends choosing a margarine in tub or liquid form that contains no more than two grams of saturated fat per tablespoon and has liquid vegetable oil listed as the first ingredient.

RECIPES GALORE AND SO MUCH MORE

OUR BEST LOW-FAT, LOW-CALORIE RECIPES is full of good things that will please your family and simplify your life. Here's a peek.

☀ **Over 300 Flavor-Packed Recipes.** Only the best-tasting light recipes from *Southern Living* are in this collection, ones we'd serve our own families. We've got you covered for every meal of the day and for every occasion.

☀ **Low-Fat, Low-Calorie Guarantee.** When it came to evaluating the recipes in this cookbook, choosing ones low in fat wasn't enough. Research shows that you should keep an eye on calories as well as fat. You can be a guiltless gourmet when you cook with these recipes.

☀ **Menus for Entertaining.** Casual but classy is the agenda for the menus starting on page 13. Whether you dine outdoors or take a culinary excursion to another country, you'll like the simplicity of these menus. An easy game plan takes you from start to serve in a flash.

☀ **Menus for Everyday.** From meat-and-potato mainstays to hearty one-dish meals, the supper menus beginning on page 37 will become favorites you'll make again and again. An equipment list and a game plan keep preparation simple.

☀ **Meals in Minutes.** Flip to page 59 when time *isn't* on your side. Ten menus feature quick entrée recipes and suggestions for no-recipe-needed side dishes and desserts. The best part? Everything's ready, start to finish, in just 30 to 45 minutes. This is our favorite chapter!

☀ **Up-to-Date Nutritional Analyses.** With each recipe, you'll find a nutritional analysis per serving. Listed first are the calories per serving and percent of those calories that come from fat. Also included are values for total grams of fat (with saturated, monounsaturated, and polyunsaturated breakdowns), cholesterol, sodium, carbohydrate, fiber, and protein.

☀ **Nearly 100 Photographs.** You'll be able to see just what many of these recipes look like—over a fourth of them have beautiful full-color photos. You'll also learn lots of easy garnishing ideas.

☀ **A Peek at Our Ultimate Favorite Recipes.** In a big hurry? Want to impress the boss or a new beau? See the facing page for our top choices to ensure culinary success.

☀ **An Easy-to-Use Index.** Cross-referenced by type of food and particular ingredient, this handy index quickly puts hundreds of recipes at your fingertips.

AND THE WINNERS ARE . . .

Here they are — our top picks! After testing and tasting over 300 recipes for the book, these are the ones our foods editors selected as the cream of the crop.

Quickest Recipes

■ **Bean and Hominy Soup**, page 61, so simple to throw together

■ **Fettuccine Primavera**, page 126, a mélange of tender pasta and fresh vegetables
■ **Potato-Corn Chowder**, page 164, a sure-fire way to warm up on a cold winter's day
■ **Roast and Relish Sandwiches**, page 172, to satisfy even the heartiest appetites

page 164

Most Sinful Desserts

■ **Spice Cake with Coffee Frosting**, page 224, stately and elegant
■ **Strawberry Yogurt Layer Cake**, page 226, a cool summer treat so pretty in pink
■ **Chocolate-Almond Cheesecake**, page 227, our ultimate favorite dessert
■ **Old-Fashioned Banana Pudding**, page 228, just like Mom used to make

page 228

Outstanding Make-Aheads

■ **Frozen Chocolate Brownie Pie**, page 31, a frosty treat you can't resist

■ **Grilled Turkey Breast with Cranberry Salsa**, page 108, perfect for company
■ **Black Bean Salad**, page 137, a spicy south-of-the-border side
■ **Tropical Gazpacho**, page 151, a cool fruit soup guaranteed to beat the heat

page 31

Most Decadent Recipes

■ **Spicy Beef Chimichangas**, page 99, a sure-fire family favorite
■ **Southern-Style Creamed Corn**, page 190, tastier than the original
■ **Old-Fashioned Cinnamon Rolls**, page 211, packed with cinnamon and dripping with glaze
■ **Light Hummingbird Cake**, page 225, a light version of our most requested recipe

Menus

MEALS FOR ENTERTAINING

*P*lanning a dinner party or a birthday celebration? You'll find just what to serve with these fuss-free entertaining menus. And you can work magic in your kitchen with our planning and organizing tips. Choose from menus created from top-rated recipes, and get things to the table on time with helpful menu plans. There's even a list of equipment you'll need to prepare each meal. But don't wait for a special occasion to savor these menus. Any meal becomes an occasion when you serve favorites like Grilled Chicken and Vegetable Salad and Frozen Chocolate Brownie Pie from *Summer Get-Together.*

Grilled Chicken and Vegetable Salad and Whole Wheat Roll (Menu begins on page 27.)

Alfresco Summer Supper

✺

Apricot-Mint Cooler

Grilled Tuna with Poblano Salsa

Yellow Rice

Grilled Zucchini Slices

Strawberries Marsala

Serves 4
678 calories per serving (11% from fat)

*L*ike to entertain, but hate to heat up the kitchen? Consider cooking on the grill — it's the easiest way to go, especially when dining outdoors. To keep things simple, slice two medium zucchini diagonally for four servings, and grill alongside the tuna. Serve Strawberries Marsala for dessert, lingering with your guests to bring this summer evening to a pleasant end.

Equipment Needed
- Grill with lid
- Large nonstick skillet with lid
- Baking sheet
- Wire-mesh strainer
- Basting brush
- Grater or zester
- Pitcher

Menu Plan
1 Prepare Strawberries Marsala 8 hours before serving; cover and chill.
2 Prepare Apricot-Mint Cooler and Poblano Salsa; cover and chill.
3 Prepare Yellow Rice; keep warm.
4 While rice cooks, grill tuna steaks and zucchini slices.

Grilled Tuna with Poblano Salsa, Yellow Rice, grilled zucchini slices (Recipes begin on next page.)

Apricot-Mint Cooler

Per serving:
Calories 159 (0% from fat)
Fat 0.0g (sat 0.0g;
    mono 0.0g; poly 0.0g)
Cholesterol 0mg
Sodium 6mg
Carbohydrate 39.6g
Fiber 0.0g
Protein 1.0g

1⅓ cups boiling water
3 tablespoons sugar
6 sprigs fresh mint, chopped
½ cup fresh lemon juice

¼ cup fresh lime juice
2 (11.5-ounce) cans apricot nectar
Garnish: fresh mint sprigs

Combine first 3 ingredients; stir until sugar dissolves. Cover; let stand 1 hour.

Pour mixture through a wire-mesh strainer into a pitcher, discarding chopped mint; stir in lemon juice, lime juice, and nectar. Cover and chill. Serve over ice. Garnish, if desired. Yield: 4 (1¼-cup) servings.

Grilled Tuna with Poblano Salsa

A south-of-the-border salsa lends just the right tang to this highly rated recipe.

Per serving:
Calories 223 (29% from fat)
Fat 7.2g (sat 1.6g;
    mono 2.7g; poly 1.9g)
Cholesterol 43mg
Sodium 347mg
Carbohydrate 11.5g
Fiber 2.1g
Protein 28.7g

2 tablespoons lime juice
1 teaspoon olive oil
4 (4-ounce) tuna steaks

Vegetable cooking spray
Poblano Salsa

Combine lime juice and oil; brush over fish.

Coat grill rack with cooking spray; place on grill over medium-hot coals (350° to 400°). Place fish on rack; grill, covered, 5 minutes on each side or until fish flakes easily when tested with a fork. Serve fish with Poblano Salsa. Yield: 4 servings.

Poblano Salsa

4 medium-size poblano chile
    peppers
2 small fresh tomatillos
1 small serrano chile pepper or
    jalapeño pepper, seeded and
    diced
½ cup chopped tomato

¼ cup diced onion
2 tablespoons chopped fresh
    cilantro or parsley
2 tablespoons lime juice
½ teaspoon salt
½ teaspoon ground cumin

Cut poblano chiles in half lengthwise; remove and discard seeds and membranes. Place poblano chile halves, skin sides up, on an aluminum foil-lined baking sheet; flatten with hand. Broil 5½ inches from heat (with electric oven door partially opened) 12 to 15 minutes or until blackened.

Plunge chile halves into ice water to cool. Remove from water; peel and discard skins. Dice chile halves.

Remove and discard tomatillo husks; wash tomatillos, and dice. Combine diced poblano chile, tomatillo, serrano chile pepper, and remaining ingredients. Cover and chill thoroughly. Yield: 1⅔ cups.

Yellow Rice

Onion, turmeric, and a bay leaf punch up the flavor of plain rice.

Olive oil-flavored vegetable
   cooking spray
¼ cup diced onion
2 cups canned no-salt-added
   chicken broth, undiluted

1 cup long-grain rice, uncooked
¼ teaspoon salt
⅛ teaspoon ground turmeric
1 bay leaf

Coat a large nonstick skillet with cooking spray; place over medium-high heat until hot. Add onion; cook, stirring constantly, until tender. Stir in broth and remaining ingredients; bring to a boil. Cover, reduce heat, and simmer 25 minutes or until rice is tender and liquid is absorbed. Remove and discard bay leaf. Yield: 4 (¾-cup) servings.

Per serving:
Calories 185 (2% from fat)
Fat 0.5g (sat 0.1g;
   mono 0.1g; poly 0.1g)
Cholesterol 0mg
Sodium 152mg
Carbohydrate 38.7g
Fiber 0.6g
Protein 3.6g

Strawberries Marsala

*Sweet and succulent wine-kissed strawberries provide
the perfect ending to this supper under the stars.*

1½ tablespoons Marsala
2 teaspoons sugar
¼ teaspoon lemon juice
4 cups fresh whole strawberries,
   hulled and halved

Garnishes: grated lemon zest,
   fresh mint sprigs

Combine first 3 ingredients in a large bowl; add strawberry halves, and toss gently. Cover and chill 8 hours, tossing occasionally.

To serve, gently toss strawberry mixture, and spoon evenly into four individual dessert dishes. Garnish, if desired. Yield: 4 (1-cup) servings.

Per serving:
Calories 51 (7% from fat)
Fat 0.4g (sat 0.0g;
   mono 0.1g; poly 0.2g)
Cholesterol 0mg
Sodium 2mg
Carbohydrate 10.7g
Fiber 3.1g
Protein 0.7g

Sunset Dinner

❋

Marinated Flank Steaks
Roasted New Potatoes
Asparagus Vinaigrette
Dinner Rolls
Lemon Angel Rolls with Raspberry Sauce

Serves 8
799 calories per serving (20% from fat)

*W*hether you're dining indoors or outside, enjoy the beauty of the sunset while
you and your guests savor this impressive
feast. Ease and simplicity are bonuses with
this mostly make-ahead menu. The calories
per serving include one dinner roll in addition to the recipes in the menu.

Equipment Needed

- Dutch oven
- Large saucepan with lid
- Small saucepan
- Broiler pan with rack
- Large baking sheet
- Two large shallow
  baking dishes
- Electric blender or
  food processor
- Rolling pin
- Pastry brush
- Basting brush
- Wire-mesh strainer
- Small jar with lid

Menu Plan

1 Marinate flank steaks 8 to 12 hours in advance.
2 Prepare Lemon Angel Rolls and Raspberry
  Sauce; cover and chill separately.
3 Prepare Asparagus Vinaigrette; cover and chill.
4 Prepare potatoes. While potatoes roast, grill
  steaks, and heat rolls.
5 Assemble dessert just before serving.

Lemon Angel Rolls with Raspberry Sauce (page 21)

19

Flavors of the Orient

❋

Hot-and-Sour Soup

Chinese Pork Tenderloins

Vegetable-Rice Toss

Almond Cookies

Green Tea

Serves 8
522 calories per serving (22% from fat)

Take a culinary excursion to the Orient the next time company comes for dinner. Our version of classic Hot-and-Sour Soup gets the evening off to an exotic start, while Almond Cookies and a sip of soothing green tea (¾ cup per serving) make a memorable finale.

Equipment Needed

- 2-quart saucepan
- Small saucepan
- Large nonstick skillet with lid
- Broiler pan with rack
- Cookie sheet
- Electric mixer
- Meat thermometer
- Basting brushes
- Wire racks

Menu Plan

1 Prepare Almond Cookies a day ahead.
2 Marinate tenderloins 3 to 8 hours.
3 Cut up vegetables for Vegetable-Rice Toss; cover and chill.
4 Broil tenderloins, and let stand 10 minutes before slicing. As soon as tenderloins go into oven, prepare Vegetable-Rice Toss; keep warm.
5 While rice cooks, prepare soup.
6 Brew green tea just before serving.

Chinese Pork Tenderloin, Vegetable-Rice Toss (Recipes begin on next page.)

Summer Get-Together

Bellini Spritzers
Grilled Chicken and Vegetable Salad
Whole Wheat Rolls
Frozen Chocolate Brownie Pie

Serves 6
805 calories per serving (15% from fat)

Summer is the perfect season for a carefree party. And with this luncheon or supper menu, relaxation is the name of the game since most of the recipes can be made ahead. Bellini Spritzers begin the celebration. You may also want to have extra sparkling mineral water on hand. After guests savor the hearty main-dish salad and tender rolls (one per serving), they can cap off the meal with frosty slices of brownie pie.

Frozen Chocolate Brownie Pie (page 31)

Equipment Needed

- Grill with lid
- Large saucepan
- Small saucepan
- 9-inch springform pan
- Muffin pans
- Electric blender or food processor
- Electric mixer
- Steamer basket
- Rolling pin
- Basting brush
- Jar with lid
- Large pitcher
- Wire rack

Menu Plan

1 Prepare pie up to a month in advance; cover and freeze until serving time.
2 Prepare roll dough up to a day ahead, if following make-ahead directions. Cover and chill.
3 Marinate chicken, steam asparagus, and prepare dressing for salad; cover and chill.
4 If you didn't prepare rolls in advance, do so at this point, allowing time for rising.
5 Shape and bake rolls at serving time. While they bake, grill chicken, and assemble salad.
6 Prepare spritzers just before serving.

Whole Wheat Rolls

Serve these tender spirals of fragrant yeast bread hot from the oven.

2 packages active dry yeast
1¾ cups warm water (105° to 115°)
¼ cup vegetable oil
1 egg
2¼ cups whole wheat flour

⅓ cup sugar
1½ teaspoons salt
2¾ to 3¼ cups all-purpose flour
3 tablespoons all-purpose flour
Butter-flavored vegetable cooking spray

Combine yeast and warm water in a 2-cup liquid measuring cup; let stand 5 minutes.

Combine yeast mixture, oil, and next 4 ingredients in a large mixing bowl; beat at medium speed of an electric mixer 2 minutes. Gradually stir in enough of 2¾ to 3¼ cups all-purpose flour to make a soft dough.

Sprinkle 3 tablespoons flour evenly over work surface. Turn dough out onto floured surface, and knead until smooth and elastic (about 5 minutes). Place in a bowl coated with cooking spray, turning to coat top. Cover and let rise in a warm place (85°), free from drafts, 1 hour or until doubled in bulk.

Punch dough down; cover and let rise in a warm place, free from drafts, 20 minutes or until doubled in bulk.

Punch dough down; divide in half. Roll each half into a 14- x 9-inch rectangle. Cut each rectangle of dough in half crosswise; cut each half into 9 (1-inch-wide) strips. Roll each strip, jellyroll fashion, into a spiral; place in muffin pans coated with cooking spray. Coat rolls with cooking spray. Let rise, uncovered, in a warm place, free from drafts, 40 minutes or until doubled in bulk. Bake rolls at 400° for 10 to 12 minutes or until golden. Yield: 3 dozen.

Note: To make rolls ahead, prepare dough as directed, turning out onto floured surface and kneading until smooth and elastic (about 5 minutes). Place dough in a bowl coated with cooking spray, turning to coat top. Cover and chill 8 hours or overnight. Punch dough down; divide in half. Roll out, shape, and bake as directed.

Frozen Chocolate Brownie Pie

Your guests will never believe that this frozen fantasy is actually healthy.

¼ cup margarine
⅔ cup firmly packed brown sugar
½ cup egg substitute
¼ cup nonfat buttermilk
⅓ cup cocoa
¼ cup all-purpose flour
¼ teaspoon salt
1 teaspoon vanilla extract

Vegetable cooking spray
½ gallon vanilla nonfat frozen
    yogurt, softened and divided
1 quart chocolate nonfat frozen
    yogurt, softened
¾ cup lite chocolate syrup
Garnish: fresh strawberry halves

Per serving:
Calories 295 (13% from fat)
Fat 4.2g (sat 1.0g;
   mono 1.7g; poly 1.2g)
Cholesterol 0mg
Sodium 257mg
Carbohydrate 63.4g
Fiber 0.1g
Protein 9.1g

Melt margarine in a large saucepan over medium heat; add brown sugar, stirring until dissolved. Remove from heat; cool slightly.

Add egg substitute and buttermilk to margarine mixture; stir well. Combine cocoa, flour, and salt; add to buttermilk mixture, stirring until blended. Stir in vanilla. Pour batter into a 9-inch springform pan lightly coated with cooking spray. Bake at 350° for 15 minutes. Cool in pan on a wire rack.

Spread half of vanilla frozen yogurt over cooled brownie layer; freeze at least 30 minutes or until firm.

Spread chocolate frozen yogurt over vanilla frozen yogurt; freeze at least 30 minutes or until firm.

Spread remaining vanilla frozen yogurt over chocolate frozen yogurt. Cover and freeze at least 8 hours. Cut pie into 12 wedges; drizzle each serving with 1 tablespoon chocolate syrup. Garnish, if desired. Yield: 12 servings.

Fiesta Olé

❋

Mock Margaritas
Tortilla Chips and Salsa
Chicken Enchiladas
Southwestern Rice
Jicama-Orange Salad

Serves 8
675 calories per serving (17% from fat)

*L*ooking for an excuse to have a few friends over? Celebrate Cinco de Mayo (the "fifth of May") with this Mexican independence day feast. Kick off the fiesta with margaritas and crispy no-oil tortilla chips and spicy salsa. Calories per serving include 12 chips and ¼ cup salsa in addition to the recipes. And don't forget to hang a piñata for some after-dinner fun.

Equipment Needed
- Large saucepan with lid
- Small saucepan
- Large nonstick skillet
- Small skillet
- Electric blender
- 13- x 9- x 2-inch baking dish
- Large freezer container
- Jar with lid

Menu Plan
1 Prepare frozen portion of margaritas.
2 Prepare oranges, jicama, red pepper, and dressing for salad; cover and chill.
3 Cook chicken. Assemble enchilada ingredients.
4 Remove margarita mixture from freezer, and let stand 30 minutes before serving.
5 Prepare Southwestern Rice; keep warm.
6 While rice cooks, prepare enchiladas.
7 Assemble Jicama-Orange Salad.

Chicken Enchilada, Southwestern Rice (Recipes begin on next page.)

MEALS FOR EVERYDAY

*W*hat's for supper? It's a nightly question that can strike fear in the heart of the family chef. Now there's no need to fret when you've got these easy menus. Add a little spice to suppertime with Chicken and Sausage Jambalaya from *Supper on the Bayou* or Seafood Gumbo from the *Cajun Feast* menu. Or give chicken a rest, and try Honey-Grilled Pork Chops from *Dinner on the Deck*. Follow the game plan that accompanies each menu, and you'll be calm, cool, and collected the next time somebody barrels through the door asking, "What's for supper?"

Honey-Grilled Pork Chops, roasted potato wedges, and Red Cabbage and Apple Slaw (Menu begins on page 47.)

Cajun Feast

※

Mixed Green Salad
Seafood Gumbo
French Bread
Bread Pudding with Whiskey Sauce

Serves 8
668 calories per serving (10% from fat)

*Y*our family will sing the praises of Louisiana cooking after just one taste of this gumbo. With four kinds of seafood and lots of veggies, this dish is chock-full of good things. For each person, serve the gumbo with a one-inch slice of French bread and one cup mixed salad greens topped with one tablespoon fat-free Italian dressing. No matter what the occasion, this menu is sure to be requested often.

Equipment Needed

- Dutch oven
- Large saucepan with lid (for rice)
- Small saucepan
- 15- x 10- x 1-inch jellyroll pan
- Large baking sheet
- Large shallow pan
- Eight 6-ounce custard cups
- Wire whisk

Menu Plan

1 Prepare Seafood Gumbo; cook rice for gumbo.
2 While rice cooks, toast bread cubes for bread pudding, prepare salad, and, if desired, heat French bread.
3 Assemble bread pudding, and place in oven to bake just before serving dinner.
4 Prepare Whiskey Sauce to top bread pudding just before serving.

Seafood Gumbo (next page), French bread

A Family Affair

※

Stuffed Flank Steak with Fettuccine
Snow Peas with Sweet Red Pepper
Peach Sherbet

Serves 6
608 calories per serving (22% from fat)

*C*elebrate a special family occasion with this festive menu. The recipes call for no season-specific ingredients, so they're perfect for any time of year. Even the sherbet gives you the option of using fresh or frozen peaches. But during the summer, use fresh peaches, and make plenty to keep in the freezer—you'll have instant refreshment for hot summer days.

Equipment Needed

- Dutch oven (for fettuccine)
- Large nonstick skillet
- Medium saucepan
- 13- x 9- x 2-inch pan
- 8-inch square pan
- Food processor
- String

Menu Plan

1 Make Peach Sherbet up to one month in advance.
2 Prepare and bake Stuffed Flank Steak.
3 Cook fettuccine, and make sauce to serve over steak while steak stands 15 minutes; keep warm.
4 Prepare Snow Peas with Sweet Red Pepper, and slice steak just before serving.
5 Remove sherbet from freezer 10 minutes before serving.

Stuffed Flank Steak with Fettuccine, Snow Peas with Sweet Red Pepper (Recipes begin on next page.)

Dinner on the Deck

Honey-Grilled Pork Chops
Roasted Potato Wedges
Red Cabbage and Apple Slaw
Fresh Fruit with Mint-Balsamic Tea

Serves 6
566 calories per serving (25% from fat)

*S*it back and enjoy nature's ambience by dining on the deck—just the place for a relaxing dinner. With minimal planning, you can prepare most of this meal earlier in the afternoon. Then just transfer this no-fuss fare from the kitchen to the deck, and relish the calm of the evening. The calories per serving reflect half of an eight-ounce baking potato cut into four wedges, in addition to the other menu items.

Equipment Needed

- Large shallow dish
- Small saucepan
- Grill with lid
- Baking sheet (for potato wedges)
- Wire whisk
- Medium saucepan
- Wire-mesh strainer
- Basting brush

Menu Plan

1 Marinate pork chops. While chops marinate, make slaw and Fresh Fruit with Mint-Balsamic Tea; cover and chill separately.
2 Coat potato wedges with vegetable cooking spray. Roast in a single layer on a large baking sheet at 400° for about 40 minutes or until browned, turning once.
3 While potato wedges roast, grill pork chops.

Fresh Fruit with Mint-Balsamic Tea (page 49)

Hot off the Grill

Citrus-Ginger Chicken
Pretty Pepper Kabobs
Whole Wheat Dinner Rolls
Spiced Peaches with Nutty Dumplings

Serves 4
468 calories per serving (20% from fat)

This quick menu puts the grill and your outdoor cooking skills to good use. Grill the chicken breasts and pepper kabobs side by side in a matter of minutes. Complete the meal with one dinner roll per person (you'll find a recipe on page 30) and a generous serving of this quick take on a summery peach cobbler.

Equipment Needed

- Grill with lid
- Medium saucepan with lid
- Eight 6-inch wooden skewers
- Basting brush

Menu Plan

1 Soak wooden skewers in water 30 minutes. Assemble Pretty Pepper Kabobs.
2 Combine peach portion of Spiced Peaches with Nutty Dumplings; set aside.
3 Grill Citrus-Ginger Chicken. After chicken grills 10 minutes, place pepper kabobs on grill with chicken.
4 Heat rolls while chicken and kabobs grill.
5 Heat peach mixture, and prepare dumpling mixture for the dessert when ready to serve; cook dumplings in boiling peach mixture.

Citrus-Ginger Chicken, Pretty Pepper Kabobs, whole wheat dinner rolls (Recipes begin on next page.)

51

Supper on the Bayou

☀

Chicken and Sausage Jambalaya

Mixed Green Salad

Cornmeal Muffins

Bananas Foster

Serves 6
662 calories per serving (16% from fat)

*S*upper for last-minute weeknight guests is a snap when the menu includes a hearty one-dish meal like Chicken and Sausage Jambalaya. It looks impressive, but it's a cinch to prepare. A mixed green salad (one cup mixed greens with one tablespoon fat-free Italian dressing per serving) and a quick bread like Cornmeal Muffins (one per serving) are all you need to complete the menu.

Equipment Needed
- Dutch oven with lid
- Muffin pans
- Large skillet

Menu Plan
1 Prepare salad; cover and chill.
2 Prepare Chicken and Sausage Jambalaya.
3 While jambalaya cooks, bake Cornmeal Muffins.
4 Prepare Bananas Foster just before serving.

Chicken and Sausage Jambalaya, mixed green salad, Cornmeal Muffin (Recipes begin on next page.)

MEALS IN MINUTES

*I*f a busy schedule leaves you with only 30 minutes to get a meal on the table, then we're here to lend a hand. Each of these menus features an almost effortless entrée, along with one or two simple side dishes that don't even need recipes. The menus are so quick and easy, you'll probably have enough time to whip up a dessert, too. Our editors' favorites? We especially like Bean and Hominy Soup from *Soup and Salad* and Hoisin Pork Medaillons from *Company's Coming.*

Hoisin Pork Medaillons and steamed carrot sticks (page 67)

Fish Feast

Grilled Marinated Grouper

Baked Potatoes

Steamed Fresh Broccoli

Vanilla Frozen Yogurt with
Gingersnaps

Serves 4
643 calories per serving (20% from fat)

Calories per serving include 1 serving grouper,
1 (8-ounce) potato, 1 cup broccoli, and ½ cup
frozen yogurt with 3 gingersnaps.

Grilled Marinated Grouper

Per serving:
Calories 170 (42% from fat)
Fat 8.0g (sat 1.2g;
   mono 5.2g; poly 0.9g)
Cholesterol 42mg
Sodium 208mg
Carbohydrate 1.4g
Fiber 0.1g
Protein 22.1g

1 (1-pound) grouper fillet, cut
   into 4 pieces
½ teaspoon grated lemon rind
3 tablespoons fresh lemon juice
1 teaspoon prepared horseradish
¼ teaspoon dried oregano

¼ teaspoon dried basil
¼ teaspoon salt
⅛ teaspoon pepper
1 small clove garlic, halved
2 tablespoons olive oil
Vegetable cooking spray

Arrange fish in a shallow dish. Combine lemon rind and next 7 ingredients in
container of an electric blender. Cover and process 20 seconds. With blender
running, add oil in a slow stream. Pour mixture over fish, and turn to coat.
Cover and marinate in refrigerator 8 hours, turning fish occasionally.

Remove fish from marinade. Place marinade in a saucepan; bring to a boil.
Remove from heat. Coat grill rack with cooking spray; place on grill over
medium-hot coals (350° to 400°). Arrange fish in a grill basket coated with
cooking spray. Grill, covered, 7 to 8 minutes on each side or until fish flakes
easily when tested with a fork. Baste with marinade. Yield: 4 servings.

Patio Supper

※

Herbed Catfish Fillets

Tomato Slices on Lettuce

Soft Breadsticks

Watermelon

Serves 4
317 calories per serving (24% from fat)

Calories per serving include 1 serving catfish,
2 tomato slices on 2 lettuce leaves,
2 breadsticks, and 3 cups cubed watermelon.

Herbed Catfish Fillets

½ cup fine, dry breadcrumbs
¼ cup all-purpose flour
1 tablespoon chopped fresh
    parsley or 1 teaspoon dried
    parsley flakes
1½ teaspoons chopped fresh
    dillweed or ½ teaspoon
    dried dillweed
1½ teaspoons chopped fresh
    thyme or ½ teaspoon
    dried thyme

2 teaspoons chicken-flavored
    bouillon granules
1 teaspoon dried onion flakes
1 teaspoon paprika
¼ teaspoon garlic powder
4 (4-ounce) farm-raised catfish
    fillets
Butter-flavored vegetable cooking
    spray
Garnish: fresh thyme sprigs

※ Per serving:
Calories 227 (27% from fat)
Fat 6.7g (sat 1.5g;
    mono 2.1g; poly 1.4g)
Cholesterol 66mg
Sodium 635mg
Carbohydrate 17.0g
Fiber 1.0g
Protein 23.6g

Combine first 9 ingredients. Coat fish with cooking spray; dredge in bread-crumb mixture. Place fish on rack of a broiler pan coated with cooking spray. Bake at 400° for 20 minutes or until fish flakes easily when tested with a fork. Garnish, if desired. Yield: 4 servings.

Summer Repast

Favorite Crab Cakes

Corn on the Cob

Mixed Green Salad

Angel Food Cake with
Strawberries

Serves 4
303 calories per serving (16% from fat)

Calories per serving include 2 crab cakes,
1 medium ear corn, 1 cup salad with
1 tablespoon fat-free salad dressing, and
1 (2-inch) slice cake with ½ cup berries.

Favorite Crab Cakes

Mild crabmeat teams perfectly with bold seasonings in these tender morsels.

Per serving:
Calories 155 (25% from fat)
Fat 4.3g (sat 0.3g;
    mono 0.3g; poly 0.8g)
Cholesterol 112mg
Sodium 990mg
Carbohydrate 2.3g
Fiber 0.1g
Protein 24.3g

2 egg whites, lightly beaten
2 tablespoons reduced-calorie
    mayonnaise
2 teaspoons chopped fresh parsley
1¼ teaspoons Old Bay seasoning
1 teaspoon low-sodium
    Worcestershire sauce
1 teaspoon dry mustard

¼ teaspoon pepper
½ cup soft breadcrumbs
1 pound fresh lump crabmeat,
    drained
Olive oil-flavored vegetable
    cooking spray
¼ cup fat-free tartar sauce
Garnish: fresh parsley sprigs

Combine first 7 ingredients; stir in breadcrumbs and crabmeat. Shape mixture
into 8 (2½-inch) patties.

Coat a large nonstick skillet with cooking spray; place over medium-high
heat until hot. Add patties; cook 3 minutes on each side or until browned.
Serve patties with tartar sauce. Garnish, if desired. Yield: 4 servings.

Sunday Supper

Beef Hash

Iceberg Lettuce Wedges with French Dressing

Chocolate Pudding

Serves 2

533 calories per serving (20% from fat)

Calories per serving include 1 serving hash,
1 (2-inch) wedge lettuce with 1 tablespoon fat-free
French dressing, and ¹/₂ cup instant
chocolate pudding prepared with skim milk.

Beef Hash

Vegetable cooking spray
2 teaspoons vegetable oil
1¹/₄ cups peeled, cubed, cooked potato
1 cup cubed, cooked lean beef
¹/₂ cup chopped onion
¹/₃ cup skim milk
¹/₄ cup low-sodium beef broth, undiluted

¹/₄ teaspoon salt
¹/₄ teaspoon pepper
1 tablespoon chopped fresh parsley
1 (6-inch) French roll, split and toasted

Per serving:
Calories 382 (26% from fat)
Fat 11.0g (sat 3.2g;
    mono 4.1g; poly 2.9g)
Cholesterol 55mg
Sodium 744mg
Carbohydrate 47.8g
Fiber 3.0g
Protein 23.0g

Coat a medium nonstick skillet with cooking spray; add oil. Place skillet over medium-high heat until hot. Add potato, beef, and onion; cook 10 minutes or until potato is browned and onion is tender, stirring occasionally.

Add milk and next 3 ingredients. Reduce heat; simmer, uncovered, 5 to 10 minutes or until desired consistency, stirring occasionally. Stir in parsley. Spoon hash evenly over roll halves. Yield: 2 servings.

Fireside Supper

Easy Weeknight Chili

Corn Muffins

Pound Cake with
Vanilla Frozen Yogurt

Serves 6
562 calories per serving (19% from fat)

Calories per serving include 1 serving chili,
1 muffin, and 1 (1-inch) slice fat-free pound
cake with ½ cup frozen yogurt.

Easy Weeknight Chili

Per serving:
Calories 302 (20% from fat)
Fat 6.6g (sat 2.2g;
mono 1.9g; poly 0.7g)
Cholesterol 52mg
Sodium 277mg
Carbohydrate 34.7g
Fiber 9.5g
Protein 29.0g

1 pound ground round
1¼ cups chopped onion
1¼ cups chopped green pepper
6 cloves garlic, pressed
Vegetable cooking spray
2 (14½-ounce) cans no-salt-added
   stewed tomatoes, undrained
   and chopped
1 (15-ounce) can no-salt-added
   kidney beans, drained

1 (8-ounce) can no-salt-added
   tomato sauce
1 (1-ounce) envelope onion soup mix
1 cup water
3 tablespoons chili powder
1 tablespoon paprika
1¼ teaspoons hot sauce
¼ cup plus 2 tablespoons (1½
   ounces) shredded reduced-fat
   sharp Cheddar cheese

Cook first 4 ingredients in a Dutch oven coated with cooking spray over
medium-high heat until beef is browned, stirring until it crumbles. Drain.

Return mixture to Dutch oven; add tomato and next 7 ingredients. Bring to
a boil; cover, reduce heat, and simmer 20 minutes, stirring occasionally. Ladle
chili evenly into six bowls; top evenly with cheese. Yield: 6 (1½-cup) servings.

Company's Coming

Hoisin Pork Medaillons

Steamed Carrot Sticks

Whole Wheat Dinner Rolls

Lemon Sorbet

Serves 4
425 calories per serving (21% from fat)

Calories per serving include 1 serving
pork, ½ cup carrot sticks,
1 roll, and ½ cup sorbet.

Hoisin Pork Medaillons

1 tablespoon dark sesame oil
Vegetable cooking spray
¼ to ½ teaspoon dried crushed
   red pepper
3 cloves garlic, minced
1 (1-pound) pork tenderloin, cut
   into ½-inch slices
¼ cup plus 2 tablespoons water

⅓ cup dry sherry
3 tablespoons hoisin sauce
3 tablespoons chopped fresh
   cilantro
2 cups hot cooked long-grain rice
   (cooked without salt or fat)
¼ cup sliced green onions
Garnish: fresh cilantro sprigs

Per serving:
Calories 303 (23% from fat)
Fat 7.9g (sat 1.9g;
   mono 3.2g; poly 2.0g)
Cholesterol 79mg
Sodium 195mg
Carbohydrate 29.1g
Fiber 1.0g
Protein 27.1

Heat oil in a nonstick skillet coated with cooking spray over medium-high heat.
Add pepper and garlic; cook, stirring for 1 minute. Add pork; cook 4 minutes on
each side or until browned. Remove pork. Wipe skillet with a paper towel.

   Combine water and next 3 ingredients in skillet. Cook over medium heat,
stirring constantly, 1 minute or until thickened. Return pork to skillet; turn to
coat. Place rice on a serving platter. Spoon pork mixture over rice. Top with
green onions; garnish, if desired. Yield: 4 servings.

Weekend Finale

Wine-Poached Chicken

Hot Cooked Fettuccine

Steamed Fresh Asparagus

Fresh Melon Bowl

Serves 4
430 calories per serving (7% from fat)

Calories per serving include 1 serving chicken,
1 cup hot cooked fettuccine (cooked without
salt or fat), ¹/₄ pound steamed asparagus, and
1 cup cantaloupe and watermelon cubes.

Wine-Poached Chicken

Per serving:
Calories 147 (10% from fat)
Fat 1.6g (sat 0.4g;
    mono 0.4g; poly 0.4g)
Cholesterol 66mg
Sodium 372mg
Carbohydrate 4.7g
Fiber 0.8g
Protein 27.4g

2¹/₂ cups sliced fresh mushrooms
³/₄ cup dry white wine
2 tablespoons chopped fresh
    parsley
1¹/₂ teaspoons chopped fresh
    tarragon or ¹/₂ teaspoon
    dried tarragon

¹/₂ teaspoon salt
¹/₄ teaspoon pepper
4 (4-ounce) skinned and boned
    chicken breast halves
1 tablespoon cornstarch
2 teaspoons water
Garnish: fresh tarragon sprigs

Combine first 6 ingredients in a large nonstick skillet; bring to a boil over
high heat. Arrange chicken in a single layer in skillet; cover, reduce heat, and
simmer 20 minutes or until chicken is tender. Remove chicken from wine
mixture, and transfer to a serving platter; set aside, and keep warm.

Combine cornstarch and water; add to skillet. Bring to a boil; boil, stirring
constantly, 1 minute. Pour over chicken. Garnish, if desired. Yield: 4 servings.

Skillet Supper

Apple-Sesame Chicken Skillet

Dinner Rolls

Orange Sherbet

Serves 2
596 calories per serving (15% from fat)

Calories per serving include 1 serving chicken
skillet, 1 roll, and ½ cup sherbet.

Apple-Sesame Chicken Skillet

Pungent curry powder enhances sweet apple in this quick stir-fry.

1 tablespoon reduced-calorie
   margarine
2 (4-ounce) skinned and boned
   chicken breast halves, cut
   into thin strips
3 cups fresh broccoli flowerets
1 cup cubed Red Delicious apple
¾ cup sliced fresh mushrooms

¼ cup thinly sliced celery
1 tablespoon water
¼ teaspoon salt
¼ teaspoon curry powder
1½ cups hot cooked rice (cooked
   without salt or fat)
½ teaspoon sesame seeds, toasted

Per serving:
Calories 391 (14% from fat)
Fat 6.2g (sat 1.0g;
   mono 0.5g; poly 0.6g)
Cholesterol 66mg
Sodium 453mg
Carbohydrate 51.3g
Fiber 4.2g
Protein 33.2g

Melt margarine in a large nonstick skillet over medium-high heat; add chicken.
Cook, stirring constantly, 3 minutes. Add broccoli and next 6 ingredients;
cover, reduce heat, and simmer 5 minutes or until crisp-tender, stirring often.
   Spoon rice evenly onto two individual plates; top evenly with chicken
mixture. Sprinkle with sesame seeds. Yield: 2 servings.

RECIPES

APPETIZERS & BEVERAGES

*M*ake room for a smorgasbord of the best party starters ever—Spinach-Ricotta Phyllo Triangles, Ham-Stuffed New Potatoes, and Smoked Salmon Canapés, to name a few. We've even given you the perfect appetizer to begin an elegant dinner party—Tortellini with Rosemary-Parmesan Sauce. And don't forget the thirst quenchers. Citrus Punch and Scarlet Sipper will dispel any drought, while Hot Spiced Cider will warm you from head to toe.

Miniature Chicken Tostadas (page 85), Spinach-Stuffed Mushrooms (page 81), Apple Cooler (page 86)

73

Crudité Dip

Per tablespoon:
Calories 11 (33% from fat)
Fat 0.4g (sat 0.1g;
    mono 0.0g; poly 0.4g)
Cholesterol 1mg
Sodium 52mg
Carbohydrate 0.5g
Fiber 0.0g
Protein 1.4g

2¼ cups 1% low-fat cottage
    cheese
2½ tablespoons reduced-fat
    mayonnaise
1½ tablespoons grated Parmesan
    cheese
1½ tablespoons finely chopped
    onion

1½ tablespoons white vinegar
1½ teaspoons chopped fresh or
    frozen chives
⅛ teaspoon dried dillweed
⅛ teaspoon pepper

Position knife blade in food processor bowl; add all ingredients. Process until smooth, stopping once to scrape down sides.

Transfer dip to a serving container; cover and chill at least 1 hour. Serve with fresh raw vegetables. Yield: 3 cups.

Deviled Dip

*Pickapeppa sauce, vinegar infused with hot peppers,
is the "devil" in this dip. You'll find it alongside hot sauce
in the condiments section of your supermarket.*

Per tablespoon:
Calories 19 (47% from fat)
Fat 1.0g (sat 0.6g;
    mono 0.3g; poly 0.0g)
Cholesterol 3mg
Sodium 111mg
Carbohydrate 2.4g
Fiber 0.1g
Protein 0.3g

½ cup nonfat mayonnaise
½ cup low-fat sour cream
2 teaspoons green pepper flakes
2 teaspoons prepared mustard
2 teaspoons Pickapeppa sauce

1½ teaspoons dried onion flakes
⅛ teaspoon ground white pepper
⅛ teaspoon garlic powder
⅛ teaspoon hot sauce

Combine all ingredients; cover and chill at least 1 hour. Serve with fresh raw vegetables. Yield: 1 cup.

Creamy Ham Dip

¼ cup finely chopped celery
2½ tablespoons finely chopped onion
1½ tablespoons sweet pickle relish, drained
1 tablespoon chopped fresh parsley
3 ounces reduced-fat, low-salt, honey-flavored ham, finely chopped
1 (8-ounce) container nonfat cream cheese, softened

Per tablespoon:
Calories 14 (13% from fat)
Fat 0.2g (sat 0.1g; mono 0.0g; poly 0.0g)
Cholesterol 3mg
Sodium 90mg
Carbohydrate 0.8g
Fiber 0.0g
Protein 2.0g

Position knife blade in food processor bowl; add first 5 ingredients. Process until mixture is finely minced, stopping once to scrape down sides.

Combine ham mixture and cream cheese; cover and chill at least 1 hour. Serve with fresh raw vegetables. Yield: 1½ cups.

Fiesta Onion Salsa

The playful flavors of sweet onion, green chiles, and peppery cumin create a feisty party starter, pictured on the following page.

1 cup chopped sweet onion
¾ cup chopped tomato
1 (4.5-ounce) can chopped green chiles, drained
3 tablespoons sliced ripe olives
2 tablespoons white wine vinegar
¼ teaspoon salt
¼ teaspoon Worcestershire sauce
⅛ teaspoon ground cumin
⅛ teaspoon pepper
⅛ teaspoon hot sauce

Per tablespoon:
Calories 5 (36% from fat)
Fat 0.2g (sat 0.0g; mono 0.1g; poly 0.0g)
Cholesterol 0mg
Sodium 45mg
Carbohydrate 0.9g
Fiber 0.2g
Protein 0.1g

Combine all ingredients; cover and chill at least 2 hours. Serve salsa with no-oil-baked tortilla chips or Spicy Tortilla Chips (page 76). Yield: 2 cups.

Spicy Tortilla Chips and Fiesta Onion Salsa (previous page)

Spicy Tortilla Chips

☀ Per chip:
Calories 15 (12% from fat)
Fat 0.2g (sat 0.0g;
   mono 0.0g; poly 0.1g)
Cholesterol 0mg
Sodium 22mg
Carbohydrate 3.2g
Fiber 0.3g
Protein 0.4g

12 (6-inch) corn tortillas
½ cup lime juice
¼ cup water
½ teaspoon garlic powder

¼ teaspoon salt
⅛ teaspoon ground cumin
⅛ teaspoon ground red pepper

Cut each tortilla into 4 wedges. Combine lime juice and water. Dip wedges in lime juice mixture; drain on paper towels. Arrange wedges in a single layer on a large baking sheet. Combine garlic powder and remaining 3 ingredients; sprinkle evenly over wedges.

Bake at 350° for 12 to 14 minutes or until crisp. Transfer chips to wire racks; cool completely. Store in an airtight container. Yield: 4 dozen.

Pita Chips

You can indulge guilt free with these lemon-garlic pita chips. Each has only five calories—and no fat.

3 (6-inch) whole wheat pita bread
    rounds
Butter-flavored vegetable cooking
    spray
1 tablespoon plus ½ teaspoon
    lemon juice

1 clove garlic, pressed
1 tablespoon minced fresh parsley
1½ teaspoons minced fresh chives
¼ teaspoon salt
⅛ teaspoon pepper

Per chip:
Calories 5 (0% from fat)
Fat 0.0g (sat 0.0g;
    mono 0.0g; poly 0.0g)
Cholesterol 0mg
Sodium 16mg
Carbohydrate 1.0g
Fiber 0.1g
Protein 0.2g

Separate each pita bread round into 2 rounds; cut each round into 8 wedges. Arrange wedges, cut sides up, in a single layer on a large baking sheet. Coat wedges with cooking spray.

Combine lemon juice and garlic; lightly brush over wedges. Combine parsley and remaining 3 ingredients; sprinkle mixture evenly over wedges.

Bake at 350° for 12 minutes or until lightly browned. Transfer chips to wire racks; cool completely. Store in an airtight container. Yield: 4 dozen.

Popcorn with Pizzazz

Our cheesy seasoning blend provides a chili powder punch, so pop this corn without salt or fat.

2½ teaspoons grated Parmesan
    cheese
¾ teaspoon salt
½ teaspoon onion powder
½ teaspoon garlic powder
½ teaspoon ground thyme
½ teaspoon paprika

½ teaspoon chili powder
15 cups popped corn (popped
    without salt or fat),
    divided
Butter-flavored vegetable cooking
    spray

Per serving:
Calories 60 (29% from fat)
Fat 1.9g (sat 0.4g;
    mono 0.2g; poly 0.3g)
Cholesterol 1mg
Sodium 371mg
Carbohydrate 9.6g
Fiber 1.9g
Protein 1.9g

Combine first 7 ingredients; set aside.

Coat 5 cups popped corn with cooking spray; toss well. Sprinkle about 2 teaspoons seasoning mixture over coated corn; toss well. Place mixture in a large bowl.

Repeat procedure with remaining popped corn, cooking spray, and seasoning mixture. Serve immediately. Yield: 5 (3-cup) servings.

Fruit Kabobs with Coconut Dressing

*This creamy marmalade-kissed dressing tastes more complex
than it would seem with its three simple ingredients.*

☀ **Per serving:**
Calories 43 (13% from fat)
Fat 0.6g (sat 0.3g;
    mono 0.1g; poly 0.1g)
Cholesterol 1mg
Sodium 13mg
Carbohydrate 9.2g
Fiber 1.2g
Protein 1.1g

1½ cups vanilla low-fat yogurt
1½ tablespoons flaked coconut
1½ tablespoons low-sugar orange
    marmalade
1 medium-size Red Delicious
    apple

1 medium pear
1 tablespoon lemon juice
20 (1-inch) fresh pineapple
    chunks
20 seedless green or red grapes
20 fresh strawberries, capped

Combine first 3 ingredients; cover and chill.

Core apple and pear; cut each into 20 bite-size pieces. Toss apple and pear pieces with lemon juice.

Thread fruits alternately onto 20 (6-inch) wooden skewers. Serve kabobs with coconut dressing. Yield: 20 appetizer servings.

Marinated Artichokes

*Our test kitchens staff loves the impact fresh
herbs give this classy appetizer, but you can substitute
one-third the amount of dried herbs.*

☀ **Per serving:**
Calories 25 (4% from fat)
Fat 0.1g (sat 0.0g;
    mono 0.0g; poly 0.0g)
Cholesterol 0mg
Sodium 40mg
Carbohydrate 5.8g
Fiber 2.2g
Protein 1.5g

2 (14-ounce) cans artichoke
    hearts
3 tablespoons fresh lemon juice
1½ teaspoons sugar

1 teaspoon minced fresh oregano
1 teaspoon minced fresh tarragon
2 cloves garlic, minced
Radicchio leaves (optional)

Drain artichokes, reserving ¾ cup liquid. Quarter artichokes, and set aside.

Combine reserved artichoke liquid, lemon juice, and next 4 ingredients in a heavy-duty, zip-top plastic bag; add artichoke quarters. Seal bag, and marinate in refrigerator at least 8 hours or until ready to serve, turning bag occasionally.

To serve, drain artichoke quarters, and arrange on a serving platter or in a bowl lined with radicchio leaves, if desired. Yield: 12 appetizer servings.

Tortellini with Rosemary-Parmesan Sauce

Tortellini with Rosemary-Parmesan Sauce

2⅔ cups skim milk
2½ tablespoons nonfat dry
   milk powder
1⅔ cups nonfat cottage cheese
¼ cup grated Parmesan cheese
¼ cup chopped fresh chives
1 tablespoon lemon juice
2 teaspoons chopped fresh
   rosemary

¼ teaspoon salt
¼ teaspoon pepper
1 (9-ounce) package refrigerated
   cheese-filled tortellini (cooked
   without salt or fat)
1 (9-ounce) package refrigerated
   cheese-filled spinach tortellini
   (cooked without salt or fat)
Garnish: fresh chives

Per serving:
Calories 100 (14% from fat)
Fat 1.6g (sat 0.3g;
   mono 0.1g; poly 0.0g)
Cholesterol 2mg
Sodium 229mg
Carbohydrate 13.6g
Fiber 0.4g
Protein 8.0g

Position knife blade in food processor bowl; add skim milk and dry milk. Process 10 seconds or until blended. Add cottage cheese and next 6 ingredients; process 1 minute, stopping once to scrape down sides. Cover and chill. Serve sauce with tortellini. Garnish, if desired. Yield: 20 appetizer servings.

Ham-Stuffed New Potatoes

Ham-Stuffed New Potatoes

*Don't be daunted by dainty appetizers. Use a small spoon, even
a baby-feeding spoon, to stuff these pint-size potatoes easily.*

☀ **Per appetizer:**
Calories 51 (30% from fat)
Fat 1.7g (sat 0.8g;
 mono 0.4g; poly 0.1g)
Cholesterol 9mg
Sodium 179mg
Carbohydrate 5.2g
Fiber 0.5g
Protein 3.7g

15 new potatoes (about
 1½ pounds)
1 cup diced cooked lean ham
⅓ cup part-skim ricotta cheese

¼ cup light process cream cheese
1 tablespoon minced onion
1 tablespoon Dijon mustard
Garnish: fresh parsley leaves

Arrange potatoes in a steamer basket over boiling water; cover and steam
15 to 20 minutes or until tender. Remove potatoes from steamer; cool.
 Combine ham and next 4 ingredients; set aside.
 Scoop out centers of potatoes, using a melon-ball scoop. (Reserve potato
pulp for another use.) Spoon ham mixture evenly into potatoes. Garnish, if
desired. Yield: 15 appetizers.

Spinach-Stuffed Mushrooms

1 (10-ounce) package frozen
   chopped spinach, thawed
20 large fresh mushrooms
Vegetable cooking spray
⅓ cup plain nonfat yogurt
¼ cup grated Parmesan cheese
¼ cup diced onion
¼ cup (1 ounce) shredded
   reduced-fat Cheddar cheese

¼ cup (1 ounce) shredded
   reduced-fat Monterey Jack
   cheese
1 tablespoon sherry
¼ teaspoon salt
¼ teaspoon garlic powder
¼ teaspoon dried oregano
1 tablespoon grated Parmesan
   cheese

Per appetizer:
Calories 32 (31% from fat)
Fat 1.1g (sat 0.6g;
   mono 0.1g; poly 0.1g)
Cholesterol 3mg
Sodium 87mg
Carbohydrate 3.0g
Fiber 1.0g
Protein 2.8g

Drain spinach, and press between layers of paper towels until barely moist; set aside. Clean mushrooms with damp paper towels; remove stems. Finely chop stems; set aside.

   Coat a large nonstick skillet with cooking spray; place over medium-high heat until hot. Add mushroom caps; cook, stirring constantly, 5 minutes. Drain. Place caps on rack of a broiler pan, stem sides up; set aside.

   Combine spinach, chopped stems, yogurt, and next 8 ingredients; spoon evenly into mushroom caps. Sprinkle evenly with 1 tablespoon Parmesan cheese. Broil 5½ inches from heat (with electric oven door partially opened) 5 minutes or until thoroughly heated. Serve immediately. Yield: 20 appetizers.

Vegetable Nachos

7 (6-inch) corn tortillas
1 cup diced tomato
¼ cup diced green pepper
2 tablespoons sliced green onions
2 tablespoons chopped ripe olives
2 tablespoons chopped green
   chiles

2 teaspoons white vinegar
¼ teaspoon garlic powder
⅛ teaspoon freshly ground
   pepper
¼ cup (1 ounce) shredded
   reduced-fat sharp Cheddar
   cheese

Per appetizer:
Calories 20 (23% from fat)
Fat 0.5g (sat 0.2g;
   mono 0.2g; poly 0.1g)
Cholesterol 1mg
Sodium 31mg
Carbohydrate 3.5g
Fiber 0.5g
Protein 0.7g

Cut each tortilla into 4 wedges; arrange wedges in a single layer on a large baking sheet. Bake at 350° for 8 minutes or until crisp.

   Combine tomato and next 7 ingredients; spoon evenly onto tortilla wedges. Sprinkle evenly with cheese. Broil 5½ inches from heat (with electric oven door partially opened) 1 minute or until cheese melts. Serve immediately. Yield: 28 appetizers.

Quick Quesadillas

Speed preparation by using a large griddle to cook several quesadillas at a time.

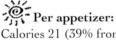 **Per wedge:**
Calories 41 (26% from fat)
Fat 1.3g (sat 0.4g;
   mono 0.0g; poly 0.0g)
Cholesterol 3mg
Sodium 142mg
Carbohydrate 4.8g
Fiber 0.4g
Protein 2.6g

¾ cup (3 ounces) shredded
   reduced-fat Monterey Jack
   cheese
¾ cup (3 ounces) shredded nonfat
   sharp Cheddar cheese

1 (4.5-ounce) can chopped green
   chiles, drained
1 cup chopped tomato
6 (6-inch) flour tortillas
Vegetable cooking spray

Divide first 4 ingredients evenly among tortillas, arranging ingredients just off center of each tortilla.

Coat a large nonstick skillet or griddle with cooking spray; place over medium-high heat until hot. Place 1 tortilla in skillet or on griddle; cook 1 minute or until bottom of tortilla is golden. Fold tortilla in half; cook 30 additional seconds or until cheeses melt. Repeat procedure with remaining tortillas. Cut each quesadilla into 4 wedges. Serve immediately. Yield: 2 dozen.

Cheese Tartlets

Per appetizer:
Calories 21 (39% from fat)
Fat 0.9g (sat 0.4g;
   mono 0.1g; poly 0.0g)
Cholesterol 2mg
Sodium 47mg
Carbohydrate 1.6g
Fiber 0.6g
Protein 1.9g

8 slices reduced-calorie wheat
   bread
¾ cup (3 ounces) shredded
   reduced-fat Swiss cheese
¼ cup grated Parmesan cheese
1 tablespoon minced fresh parsley

1 teaspoon Dijon mustard
⅛ teaspoon garlic powder
Dash of hot sauce
3 egg whites
2 tablespoons diced pimiento,
   drained

Trim crusts from bread slices. Cut each bread slice into 4 squares; gently press each square into ungreased miniature (1½-inch) muffin pans. Bake at 400° for 3 to 4 minutes or until lightly browned. Set aside.

Combine Swiss cheese and next 5 ingredients; set aside.

Beat egg whites in a large mixing bowl at high speed of an electric mixer until stiff; fold in cheese mixture. Spoon 1 teaspoon mixture into each bread shell. Bake at 400° for 6 to 8 minutes or until filling is slightly puffed.

Remove tartlets from pans; top evenly with diced pimiento. Serve immediately. Yield: 32 appetizers.

Spinach-Ricotta Phyllo Triangles

Classic Mediterranean-inspired ingredients are surrounded by flaky strips of phyllo pastry in this handheld version of the Greek spinach pie, spanakopita.

2 (10-ounce) packages frozen chopped spinach, thawed
Butter-flavored vegetable cooking spray
1 cup minced onion
⅔ cup crumbled feta cheese
⅔ cup part-skim ricotta cheese
2 tablespoons dry sherry
1 teaspoon dried oregano
½ teaspoon garlic powder
½ teaspoon salt
½ teaspoon freshly ground pepper
14 sheets frozen phyllo pastry, thawed

Per appetizer:
Calories 34 (34% from fat)
Fat 1.3g (sat 0.6g; mono 0.3g; poly 0.2g)
Cholesterol 3mg
Sodium 86mg
Carbohydrate 3.9g
Fiber 0.4g
Protein 1.5g

Drain spinach, and press between layers of paper towels until barely moist; set aside.

Coat a large nonstick skillet with cooking spray; place over medium-high heat until hot. Add onion; cook, stirring constantly, until tender. Remove from heat; stir in spinach, feta cheese, and next 6 ingredients.

Place 1 phyllo sheet on a damp towel (keep remaining phyllo sheets covered). Lightly coat phyllo sheet with cooking spray, and layer a second phyllo sheet on top of first sheet, lightly coating with cooking spray. Cut stack of phyllo sheets crosswise into 7 (2⅓-inch) strips.

Working with 1 strip at a time, place about 2 teaspoons spinach mixture at base of strip (keep remaining strips covered). Fold right bottom corner over to form a triangle. Continue folding triangle back and forth to end of strip. Repeat entire procedure with remaining 12 phyllo sheets, cooking spray, and remaining spinach mixture.

Place triangles, seam sides down, on baking sheets coated with cooking spray. Lightly coat top of each triangle with cooking spray. Bake at 350° for 25 minutes or until golden. Serve immediately. Yield: 49 appetizers.

Smoked Salmon Canapés

Smoked Salmon Canapés

16 slices party-style pumpernickel
   bread
1 (3-ounce) package thinly sliced
   smoked salmon
⅓ cup light process cream cheese,
   softened

¼ cup finely chopped green
   onions
1 teaspoon skim milk
¼ teaspoon dried dillweed
⅛ teaspoon ground white pepper
Garnish: fresh dillweed sprigs

Cut bread slices diagonally into triangles; set aside. Cut salmon crosswise
into 32 strips; set aside.

Combine cream cheese and next 4 ingredients. Spoon ½ teaspoon cream
cheese mixture onto each bread triangle; top each with a salmon strip (strips
may separate). Garnish, if desired. Yield: 32 appetizers.

Baked Oysters Italiano

3 tablespoons commercial fat-free
   Italian salad dressing
2 teaspoons lemon juice
¼ teaspoon hot sauce
2 tablespoons Italian-seasoned
   breadcrumbs
1 tablespoon grated Parmesan
   cheese

⅛ teaspoon garlic powder
⅛ teaspoon dried Italian
   seasoning
Rock salt
1 dozen fresh oysters (in the
   shell)
1 tablespoon minced fresh parsley

Per appetizer:
Calories 22 (20% from fat)
Fat 0.5g (sat 0.2g;
   mono 0.1g; poly 0.1g)
Cholesterol 8mg
Sodium 127mg
Carbohydrate 2.7g
Fiber 0.0g
Protein 1.5g

Combine first 3 ingredients; set aside. Combine breadcrumbs and next 3 ingredients; set aside.

Sprinkle a layer of rock salt in a 15- x 10- x 1-inch jellyroll pan.

Scrub oyster shells, and open; discard tops. Arrange shell bottoms (containing oysters) over salt. Spoon dressing mixture evenly over oysters, and sprinkle evenly with breadcrumb mixture. Bake at 425° for 6 to 8 minutes or until edges of oysters begin to curl. Sprinkle with parsley. Yield: 1 dozen.

Note: Skip the shell shucking, if you'd like, and bake these oysters in shell-shaped baking dishes. Use shucked oysters sold in tubs at the seafood counter.

Miniature Chicken Tostadas

1 cup finely chopped cooked
   chicken breast (skinned
   before cooking and cooked
   without salt)
½ cup finely chopped jicama
½ cup (2 ounces) shredded
   reduced-fat Cheddar cheese

¼ cup reduced-fat mayonnaise
1 tablespoon drained diced
   pimiento
1 (4.5-ounce) can chopped green
   chiles, drained
8 (6-inch) corn tortillas

Per appetizer:
Calories 25 (22% from fat)
Fat 0.6g (sat 0.2g;
   mono 0.1g; poly 0.1g)
Cholesterol 5mg
Sodium 52mg
Carbohydrate 3.0g
Fiber 0.3g
Protein 2.1g

Combine first 6 ingredients; set aside.

Cut each tortilla into 5 rounds, using a 2-inch biscuit cutter. Place rounds on a large baking sheet; bake at 350° for 6 minutes. Turn chips, and bake 2 to 3 additional minutes or until crisp.

Spread chicken mixture over chips (about 1 tablespoon per chip). Broil 5½ inches from heat (with electric oven door partially opened) 3 minutes or until mixture is hot and bubbly. Serve immediately. Yield: 40 appetizers.

Apple Cooler

Per serving:
Calories 82 (1% from fat)
Fat 0.1g (sat 0.0g;
    mono 0.0g; poly 0.0g)
Cholesterol 0mg
Sodium 5mg
Carbohydrate 20.8g
Fiber 0.5g
Protein 0.3g

2½ cups unsweetened apple juice
¼ cup lemon juice
1 (11.5-ounce) can apricot nectar

¼ teaspoon bitters (optional)
2 (6½-ounce) bottles sparkling
    water, chilled

Combine first 3 ingredients; stir in bitters, if desired. Cover and chill.
    Just before serving, stir in chilled sparkling water. Serve immediately over ice. Yield: 6 (1-cup) servings.

Note: Bitters is an alcoholic brew that imparts a bittersweet earthiness to foods.

Scarlet Sipper

Per serving:
Calories 98 (0% from fat)
Fat 0.0g (sat 0.0g;
    mono 0.0g; poly 0.0g)
Cholesterol 0mg
Sodium 20mg
Carbohydrate 24.9g
Fiber 0.1g
Protein 0.4g

4 cups cranberry-apple juice
    drink, chilled
1 cup orange juice, chilled

¼ cup lemon juice
2 (11-ounce) bottles sparkling
    water, chilled

Combine all ingredients; stir gently to combine. Serve immediately over ice. Yield: 8 (1-cup) servings.

Watermelon-Berry Slush

*This ruby slush is "berry" refreshing, especially
made with a sweet summer melon.*

Per serving:
Calories 72 (6% from fat)
Fat 0.5g (sat 0.3g;
    mono 0.1g; poly 0.0g)
Cholesterol 0mg
Sodium 18mg
Carbohydrate 16.9g
Fiber 2.7g
Protein 0.7g

4 cups seeded, cubed watermelon
1 (10-ounce) package frozen
    raspberries in light syrup

1 (11-ounce) bottle sparkling
    water

Place watermelon cubes in a single layer in a shallow pan; freeze until firm.
    Remove watermelon from freezer; let stand 5 minutes. Position knife blade in food processor bowl. Drop watermelon through food chute with processor running; process until smooth. Add chunks of frozen raspberries alternately with sparkling water, processing until mixture is smooth. Serve immediately. Yield: 5 (1-cup) servings.

Citrus Punch and Watermelon-Berry Slush (facing page)

Citrus Punch

Freeze orange juice in ice cube trays for cubes that won't water down the punch.

4 cups water, divided
¼ cup sugar
3 cups unsweetened pineapple juice
½ cup lemon juice

1 (6-ounce) can frozen orange juice concentrate, undiluted
3 (12-ounce) cans lemon-lime carbonated beverage, chilled
Garnish: lime slices

Combine 1 cup water and sugar in a small saucepan; cook over low heat until sugar dissolves, stirring occasionally. Cool. Combine sugar mixture, pineapple juice, 3 cups water, and next 2 ingredients in a bowl; cover and chill.

Just before serving, stir in carbonated beverage. Serve immediately over ice. Garnish, if desired. Yield: 13 (1-cup) servings.

Holiday Hot Fruit Punch

Per serving:
Calories 93 (2% from fat)
Fat 0.2g (sat 0.0g;
    mono 0.0g; poly 0.0g)
Cholesterol 0mg
Sodium 3mg
Carbohydrate 22.8g
Fiber 0.3g
Protein 0.6g

1 (46-ounce) can unsweetened
    apple juice
1 teaspoon ground nutmeg
1 (3-inch) stick cinnamon
2 teaspoons whole cloves
2 medium-size oranges, quartered

1 (46-ounce) can unsweetened
    pineapple juice
1 (46-ounce) can unsweetened
    orange juice
1/4 cup sugar

Combine first 3 ingredients in a Dutch oven; bring to a boil. Cover, reduce heat, and simmer 20 minutes, stirring occasionally.

Insert cloves into rinds of orange quarters; set aside.

Add pineapple juice, orange juice, and sugar to apple juice mixture; stir well. Add orange quarters. Cook 5 minutes or until mixture is thoroughly heated. (Do not boil.) Remove and discard orange quarters and cinnamon stick. Serve warm. Yield: 23 (3/4-cup) servings.

Note: Plug in a large percolator to keep this beverage warm during a party.

Hot Spiced Cider

Per serving:
Calories 112 (2% from fat)
Fat 0.2g (sat 0.1g;
    mono 0.0g; poly 0.1g)
Cholesterol 0mg
Sodium 7mg
Carbohydrate 28.0g
Fiber 1.3g
Protein 0.3g

8 cups unsweetened apple cider
1 1/2 cups water
1 teaspoon whole allspice
16 whole cloves

2 (2-inch) sticks cinnamon
1 medium-size orange, sliced
Additional cinnamon sticks
    (optional)

Combine first 6 ingredients in a 4-quart saucepan; bring to a boil. Reduce heat, and simmer 15 minutes, stirring occasionally.

Remove and discard spices and orange slices. Serve cider warm with cinnamon-stick stirrers, if desired. Yield: 9 (1-cup) servings.

Hot Cranberry Cocktail

1 tablespoon whole cloves
2 teaspoons whole allspice
3 cups unsweetened pineapple
   juice

1 (32-ounce) bottle cranberry
   juice drink
Cinnamon sticks (optional)

Per serving:
Calories 138 (1% from fat)
Fat 0.2g (sat 0.0g;
   mono 0.0g; poly 0.1g)
Cholesterol 0mg
Sodium 6mg
Carbohydrate 34.9g
Fiber 0.1g
Protein 0.4g

Cut a 6-inch square of cheesecloth; place cloves and allspice in center, and tie with string.

Combine spice bag, pineapple juice, and cranberry juice in a large saucepan. Bring to a boil; cover, reduce heat, and simmer 5 minutes. Remove and discard spice bag. Serve warm with cinnamon-stick stirrers, if desired. Yield: 7 (1-cup) servings.

Sugar-Free Hot Spiced Tea Mix

For a cozy winter gift, tuck a bag of this fragrant tea mix into a gift basket, along with a pretty mug and the hottest best-seller.

1 tablespoon plus 1 teaspoon
   ground cinnamon
2 teaspoons ground cloves
2 (1.8-ounce) containers
   sugar-free orange breakfast
   drink mix

1 (3.3-ounce) jar sugar-free,
   caffeine-free iced tea mix with
   lemon

Per serving:
Calories 11 (0% from fat)
Fat 0.0g (sat 0.0g;
   mono 0.0g; poly 0.0g)
Cholesterol 0mg
Sodium 0mg
Carbohydrate 2.2g
Fiber 0.1g
Protein 0.0g

Combine all ingredients. Store in an airtight container.

To serve, spoon 1 tablespoon mix into a cup or mug. Add 1 cup boiling water; stir until mix dissolves. Yield: about 3 cups mix or 46 (1-cup) servings.

ENTRÉES

When readers write in for recipes, their requests are frequently the same: "Give me something new for supper that my whole family will love." If this is your cry, then these recipes are for you. For intense flavor, it's hard to beat Fruit-Topped Pork Chops or Sweet-and-Sour Chicken. Need something quick? Pepper-Crusted Lamb Chops requires only six ingredients and less than 20 minutes of prep time. Looking for something a little different? Grilled Flank Steak with Corn Salsa and Shrimp Fettuccine with Dried Tomato Pesto are our top choices.

Grilled Orange Scallops (page 95)

Spicy Grilled Grouper

Fresh ginger and hot sauce add an intense flavor kick to this grilled fish. A grill basket comes in handy when grilling delicate fish because it keeps the fish from flaking apart when you turn it.

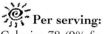 **Per serving:**
Calories 124 (19% from fat)
Fat 2.6g (sat 0.4g;
    mono 0.7g; poly 0.9g)
Cholesterol 42mg
Sodium 384mg
Carbohydrate 1.6g
Fiber 0.1g
Protein 22.7g

4 (4-ounce) grouper fillets
½ cup lemon juice
¼ cup hot sauce
2 tablespoons water
1 tablespoon plus 1 teaspoon
    grated fresh ginger

½ teaspoon salt
Vegetable cooking spray
1 tablespoon sesame seeds,
    toasted
1 tablespoon chopped fresh
    parsley

Place fillets in a single layer in a shallow dish; set aside.

Combine lemon juice and next 4 ingredients. Pour half of lemon juice mixture over fillets, turning to coat. Cover and marinate in refrigerator 1 hour, turning fillets once. Cover and chill remaining half of lemon juice mixture.

Remove fillets from marinade, discarding marinade; arrange fillets in a single layer in a grill basket coated with cooking spray. Grill, covered, over hot coals (400° to 500°) 5 minutes on each side or until fish flakes easily when tested with a fork, basting occasionally with remaining half of lemon juice mixture.

Transfer fillets to a serving plate; sprinkle with sesame seeds and parsley. Yield: 4 servings.

Steamed Orange Roughy with Herbs

Steam infuses this fish with heady aromas from fresh herb sprigs. Your choice of herbs may vary; substitute whatever is plentiful.

Per serving:
Calories 78 (9% from fat)
Fat 0.8g (sat 0.0g;
    mono 0.5g; poly 0.0g)
Cholesterol 23mg
Sodium 71mg
Carbohydrate 0.0g
Fiber 0.0g
Protein 16.7g

½ cup fresh parsley sprigs
½ cup fresh chive sprigs
½ cup fresh thyme sprigs

½ cup fresh rosemary sprigs
4 (4-ounce) orange roughy fillets
Garnish: lemon slices

Place a steamer basket over boiling water in a Dutch oven. Place half of each herb in basket. Arrange fillets over herbs in basket; top with remaining herbs.

Cover and steam 7 minutes or until fish flakes easily when tested with a fork. Remove and discard herbs. Carefully transfer fillets to a serving plate. Garnish, if desired. Yield: 4 servings.

Poached Salmon with Horseradish Sauce

Poached Salmon with Horseradish Sauce

This recipe entertains the theory that opposites attract. A dollop of creamy horseradish sauce adds a pungent kick to mild-flavored poached salmon.

¹/₄ cup nonfat mayonnaise
¹/₄ cup plain nonfat yogurt
2 teaspoons prepared horseradish
1¹/₂ teaspoons chopped fresh or
    frozen chives
1¹/₂ teaspoons lemon juice
4 cups water

1 teaspoon peppercorns
1 lemon, sliced
1 carrot, sliced
1 stalk celery, sliced
4 (4-ounce) salmon fillets
Garnishes: lemon wedges, fresh
    celery leaves

Per serving:
Calories 225 (39% from fat)
Fat 9.8g (sat 1.7g;
    mono 4.7g; poly 2.1g)
Cholesterol 77mg
Sodium 452mg
Carbohydrate 7.5g
Fiber 0.0g
Protein 25.1g

Combine first 5 ingredients. Cover and chill.

Combine water and next 4 ingredients in a large skillet; bring to a boil over medium heat. Cover, reduce heat, and simmer 10 minutes. Add salmon fillets to skillet; cover and simmer 10 minutes.

Remove skillet from heat; let stand, covered, 8 minutes. Remove fillets from skillet, transferring to individual serving plates; discard liquid and vegetables. Garnish, if desired. Serve with horseradish mixture. Yield: 4 servings.

Shrimp Fettuccine with Dried Tomato Pesto

Per serving:
Calories 459 (29% from fat)
Fat 15.0g (sat 3.5g;
   mono 5.7g; poly 2.5g)
Cholesterol 138mg
Sodium 666mg
Carbohydrate 48.3g
Fiber 0.3g
Protein 31.7g

1 pound unpeeled medium-size
   fresh shrimp
Vegetable cooking spray
1 teaspoon olive oil
2 cloves garlic, minced
¼ cup dry white wine

Dried Tomato Pesto
4 cups cooked fettuccine (cooked
   without salt or fat)
¼ cup freshly grated Parmesan
   cheese

Peel shrimp, and devein, if desired.

Coat a large nonstick skillet with cooking spray, and add oil. Place over medium heat until hot. Add garlic; cook, stirring constantly, until tender. Add shrimp; cook, stirring constantly, 1 minute. Add wine; cook, stirring constantly, 3 to 4 minutes or until shrimp turn pink. Stir in Dried Tomato Pesto; cook until mixture is thoroughly heated, stirring often.

To serve, place 1 cup pasta on each individual serving plate; top evenly with shrimp mixture. Sprinkle each serving with 1 tablespoon Parmesan cheese. Yield: 4 servings.

Dried Tomato Pesto

½ cup (1 ounce) dried tomatoes
   (packed without oil)
1 cup vegetable broth, divided
½ cup fresh basil leaves
¼ cup freshly grated Parmesan
   cheese
1½ tablespoons pine nuts

1 tablespoon olive oil
¼ teaspoon salt
¼ teaspoon ground white
   pepper
1 clove garlic
1 teaspoon cornstarch

Combine tomatoes and ½ cup broth in a small saucepan; bring to a boil. Remove from heat; let stand 10 minutes.

Position knife blade in food processor bowl; add tomato mixture, basil, and next 6 ingredients. Process until smooth, stopping twice to scrape down sides. Set tomato mixture aside.

Combine remaining ½ cup vegetable broth and cornstarch in a small saucepan. Bring to a boil over medium heat, stirring constantly; boil 1 minute. Remove from heat; stir in tomato mixture. Yield: 1½ cups.

Shrimp Fettuccine with Dried Tomato Pesto (facing page)

Barbecued Shrimp

This recipe received our highest rating. We love its distinctive tangy-sweet flavor and how quick and easy it is to prepare.

24 unpeeled jumbo fresh shrimp
Vegetable cooking spray
¼ cup diced onion
½ cup reduced-calorie ketchup
2 tablespoons chopped fresh
    rosemary
1 tablespoon dry mustard
1 tablespoon brown sugar
1 tablespoon white vinegar
¼ teaspoon garlic powder
Dash of hot sauce
1 lemon, cut into 4 wedges

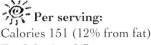 Per serving:
Calories 151 (12% from fat)
Fat 2.0g (sat 0.3g;
    mono 0.2g; poly 0.5g)
Cholesterol 221mg
Sodium 263mg
Carbohydrate 6.9g
Fiber 0.3g
Protein 24.3g

Peel shrimp, leaving tails intact. Devein shrimp, if desired. Place shrimp in a large heavy-duty, zip-top plastic bag. Set aside.

Coat a large nonstick skillet with cooking spray; place over medium-high heat until hot. Add onion; cook, stirring constantly, until tender. Stir in ketchup and next 6 ingredients; pour over shrimp. Seal bag; shake until shrimp is coated. Marinate in refrigerator 1 hour, turning bag occasionally.

Soak four 8-inch wooden skewers in water at least 30 minutes. Thread 6 shrimp onto each skewer, running skewer through neck and tail.

Coat grill rack with cooking spray; place on grill over medium-hot coals (350° to 400°). Place skewers on rack; grill, covered, 3 to 4 minutes on each side or until shrimp turn pink. Squeeze 1 lemon wedge over each skewer, and serve immediately. Yield: 4 servings.

Grilled Flank Steak with Corn Salsa

Grilled Flank Steak with Corn Salsa

*This salsa is superb. Keep it in mind for dunking no-oil
tortilla chips or for crowning any grilled meat.*

Per serving:
Calories 310 (39% from fat)
Fat 13.6g (sat 5.6g;
  mono 5.5g; poly 0.8g)
Cholesterol 60mg
Sodium 314mg
Carbohydrate 20.2g
Fiber 3.0g
Protein 25.6g

1 pound flank steak
½ cup dry red wine
¼ cup lemon juice
2 tablespoons chopped shallots
2 tablespoons Worcestershire
  sauce
1½ teaspoons pepper

3 cloves garlic, pressed
½ teaspoon garlic powder
½ teaspoon pepper
Vegetable cooking spray
Corn Salsa (facing page)
Garnishes: lime slices, fresh
  cilantro sprigs

Trim fat from steak. Make shallow cuts in steak diagonally across grain at ¾-inch intervals. Place steak in a shallow dish or heavy-duty, zip-top plastic bag.

Combine wine and next 5 ingredients; pour over steak. Cover dish, or seal bag; marinate in refrigerator 8 hours, turning steak occasionally.

Remove steak from marinade; discard marinade. Sprinkle steak with garlic powder and ½ teaspoon pepper.

Coat grill rack with cooking spray; place on grill over medium-hot coals (350° to 400°). Place steak on rack; grill, covered, 7 minutes on each side or to desired degree of doneness. Remove steak from grill; let stand 5 minutes before slicing. Cut steak diagonally across grain into thin slices; serve with Corn Salsa. Garnish, if desired. Yield: 4 servings.

Corn Salsa

1 cup fresh corn cut from cob
½ cup drained canned black
   beans
½ cup finely chopped sweet red
   pepper
2 tablespoons lime juice
2 teaspoons chopped fresh
   cilantro

¼ teaspoon salt
¼ teaspoon pepper
1 fresh jalapeño pepper, seeded
   and finely chopped
1 clove garlic, pressed

Cook corn in a small amount of boiling water 4 minutes or until crisp-tender; drain and cool. Combine corn, beans, and remaining ingredients. Cover and chill 8 hours. Yield: 2 cups.

Lemon Veal

1 tablespoon all-purpose flour
1 teaspoon beef-flavored bouillon
   granules
½ teaspoon paprika
½ teaspoon chopped fresh parsley
¼ teaspoon dried rosemary
⅛ teaspoon pepper
½ pound boneless veal round
   roast

Vegetable cooking spray
¼ cup water
¼ cup dry white wine
½ teaspoon grated lemon rind
1 tablespoon lemon juice
2 medium carrots, scraped and
   cut into thin strips
2 cups cooked long-grain rice
   (cooked without salt or fat)

Per serving:
Calories 413 (11% from fat)
Fat 5.1g (sat 1.6g;
   mono 1.2g; poly 0.4g)
Cholesterol 81mg
Sodium 249mg
Carbohydrate 58.0g
Fiber 3.0g
Protein 27.0g

Combine first 6 ingredients in a large heavy-duty, zip-top plastic bag. Trim fat from veal; cut veal into 1-inch cubes. Add veal to bag; seal bag, and shake.

Coat a large nonstick skillet with cooking spray; place over medium heat until hot. Add veal; cook, stirring constantly, until lightly browned. Add water and next 4 ingredients; bring to a boil. Cover, reduce heat, and simmer 40 minutes, stirring occasionally. To serve, spoon 1 cup rice onto each individual plate. Spoon veal mixture evenly over rice. Yield: 2 servings.

Pepper-Crusted Lamb Chops

Per serving:
Calories 304 (40% from fat)
Fat 13.5g (sat 4.5g;
    mono 5.5g; poly 1.0g)
Cholesterol 123mg
Sodium 410mg
Carbohydrate 3.2g
Fiber 0.9g
Protein 39.9g

8 (4-ounce) lean lamb loin chops
3 tablespoons coarse-grained
    mustard
1½ tablespoons cracked pepper
1½ tablespoons low-sodium soy
    sauce

2 green onions, finely chopped
2 small cloves garlic, minced
Vegetable cooking spray

Trim fat from chops. Combine mustard and next 4 ingredients; spread mixture evenly onto both sides of chops.

Coat grill rack with cooking spray; place on grill over medium-hot coals (350° to 400°). Place chops on rack; grill, uncovered, 5 to 7 minutes on each side or to desired degree of doneness. Yield: 4 servings.

Apple-Mushroom Pork Tenderloin

Apple juice concentrate imparts intense apple flavor to this tenderloin.

Per serving:
Calories 229 (13% from fat)
Fat 3.2g (sat 1.0g;
    mono 1.3g; poly 0.4g)
Cholesterol 74mg
Sodium 261mg
Carbohydrate 23.2g
Fiber 0.6g
Protein 25.6g

2 (¾-pound) pork tenderloins
½ cup all-purpose flour
½ teaspoon salt
¼ teaspoon pepper
Vegetable cooking spray

2 cups sliced fresh mushrooms
1 clove garlic, minced
¾ cup frozen unsweetened apple
    juice concentrate, thawed and
    undiluted

Trim fat from tenderloins; cut each tenderloin into 6 slices. Place slices between two sheets of heavy-duty plastic wrap; flatten to ¼-inch thickness, using a meat mallet or rolling pin.

Combine flour, salt, and pepper; dredge tenderloin slices in flour mixture.

Coat a large nonstick skillet with cooking spray; place over medium-high heat until hot. Add tenderloin slices; cook 2 to 3 minutes on each side or until browned. Remove from skillet, and set aside.

Add mushrooms and garlic to skillet; cook, stirring constantly, 1 minute. Add apple juice concentrate and tenderloin slices; bring to a boil. Reduce heat, and simmer, uncovered, 5 minutes. Yield: 6 servings.

Fruit-Topped Pork Chop

Fruit-Topped Pork Chops

Vegetable cooking spray
1 tablespoon reduced-caloric
   margarine
¼ cup chopped celery
2 tablespoons chopped onion
1 cup herb-seasoned stuffing mix
¼ cup plus 2 tablespoons chopped
   mixed dried fruit (2½ ounces)
2 tablespoons raisins

6 (4-ounce) boneless center-
   cut pork loin chops
   (¾-inch-thick)
¼ teaspoon salt
¼ teaspoon pepper
¼ cup all-purpose flour
½ cup dry white wine
Garnish: fresh sage sprigs

Per serving:
Calories 311 (36% from fat)
Fat 12.5g (sat 3.9g;
   mono 4.7g; poly 1.3g)
Cholesterol 73mg
Sodium 352mg
Carbohydrate 21.7g
Fiber 1.7g
Protein 24.6g

Coat a large nonstick skillet with cooking spray; add margarine. Place over medium-high heat until margarine melts. Add celery and onion; cook, stirring constantly, until tender. Remove from heat; add stuffing mix, dried fruit, and raisins. Toss gently to combine. Transfer mixture to a bowl; set aside.

   Sprinkle chops with salt and pepper; dredge in flour. Coat skillet with cooking spray; place over medium heat until hot. Add chops; cook until browned on both sides. Arrange chops in an 11- x 7- x 1½-inch baking dish coated with cooking spray. Spoon fruit mixture evenly over chops, and pour wine around chops. Cover and bake at 350° for 40 to 45 minutes or until chops are tender. Garnish, if desired. Yield: 6 servings.

Crispy Oven-Fried Chicken

Crispy "fried" chicken returns to the picnic basket with
this heart-healthy version of the traditional classic.

⅓ cup egg substitute
1 tablespoon water
1 cup crispy rice cereal, crushed
⅓ cup toasted wheat germ
1 tablespoon instant minced onion
½ teaspoon salt-free herb-
    and-spice blend

¼ teaspoon garlic powder
¼ teaspoon salt
¼ teaspoon pepper
1 (3-pound) broiler-fryer, cut up
    and skinned
¼ cup all-purpose flour
Vegetable cooking spray

Combine egg substitute and water in a small shallow dish. Combine cereal and next 6 ingredients in a small shallow dish. Set aside.

Combine chicken and flour in a large heavy-duty, zip-top plastic bag; seal bag, and shake until chicken is coated. Dip chicken in egg substitute mixture; dredge in cereal mixture.

Place chicken on rack of a broiler pan coated with cooking spray. Bake, uncovered, at 350° for 1 hour or until chicken is tender. Yield: 6 servings.

Chicken Pot Pie

Flaky phyllo pastry laid across the top and tucked into the sides
of this old-fashioned favorite creates a delicate, low-fat crust.

1 (3½-pound) broiler-fryer,
    skinned
2 stalks celery with leaves, cut
    into 2-inch pieces
1 large onion, cut into 6 wedges
1 bay leaf
2 quarts water
½ teaspoon pepper
3½ cups peeled, cubed baking
    potato (about 1½ pounds)

1 (16-ounce) package frozen
    mixed vegetables
1 cup skim milk
½ cup all-purpose flour
1 teaspoon salt
1 teaspoon freshly ground pepper
½ teaspoon poultry seasoning
Vegetable cooking spray
5 sheets frozen phyllo pastry,
    thawed

Combine first 6 ingredients in a Dutch oven; bring to a boil. Cover, reduce heat, and simmer 1 hour or until chicken is tender. Remove chicken from broth, reserving broth. Let chicken cool. Bone and coarsely chop chicken, and set aside.

Pour broth through a wire-mesh strainer lined with a layer of cheesecloth into a bowl, discarding solids remaining in strainer. Skim fat from broth; pour 3½ cups broth into Dutch oven. Reserve remaining broth for another use.

Add potato and frozen vegetables to Dutch oven; bring to a boil. Cover, reduce heat, and simmer 15 minutes or until vegetables are tender.

Combine milk and flour, stirring until smooth; add flour mixture to broth. Cook, stirring constantly, 1 minute or until thickened. Stir in chicken, salt, 1 teaspoon pepper, and poultry seasoning. Spoon mixture into a 13- x 9- x 2-inch baking dish coated with cooking spray; set aside.

Place 1 sheet phyllo on a damp towel; coat with cooking spray. Layer remaining 4 sheets phyllo on first sheet, coating each layer with cooking spray. Place stack of phyllo sheets on top of chicken mixture, loosely crushing edges around the dish. Bake at 400° for 15 minutes or until thoroughly heated. Let stand 10 minutes before serving. Yield: 8 servings.

Sweet-and-Sour Chicken

2 tablespoons cornstarch
2 tablespoons brown sugar
¾ teaspoon ground ginger
¼ teaspoon garlic powder
1½ cups unsweetened pineapple juice
¼ cup rice wine vinegar
¼ cup low-sodium soy sauce
¼ cup reduced-calorie ketchup
1 tablespoon low-sodium Worcestershire sauce

Vegetable cooking spray
1¼ pounds skinned and boned chicken breast halves, cut into 1-inch pieces
½ cup julienne-sliced sweet red pepper
½ cup julienne-sliced green pepper
4½ cups cooked long-grain rice (cooked without salt or fat)

Per serving:
Calories 318 (5% from fat)
Fat 1.7g (sat 0.3g; mono 0.3g; poly 0.3g)
Cholesterol 55mg
Sodium 398mg
Carbohydrate 47.9g
Fiber 1.0g
Protein 25.2g

Combine first 9 ingredients; set aside.

Coat a large nonstick skillet with cooking spray; place over medium-high heat until hot. Add chicken; cook, stirring constantly, 5 minutes. Add red and green pepper; cook, stirring constantly, 2 minutes. Gradually stir cornstarch mixture into chicken mixture. Cook over medium heat, stirring constantly, until mixture is thickened and bubbly.

To serve, spoon ¾ cup rice onto each of six individual serving plates; top evenly with chicken mixture. Yield: 6 servings.

Chicken with Tomato-Basil Pasta

Chicken with Tomato-Basil Pasta

Rolling the chicken will be easier if you layer it with a few
large basil leaves rather than a lot of small ones.

Per serving:
Calories 394 (13% from fat)
Fat 5.9g (sat 1.0g;
    mono 1.2g; poly 1.1g)
Cholesterol 72mg
Sodium 246mg
Carbohydrate 46.8g
Fiber 2.0g
Protein 34.4g

**4 (4-ounce) skinned and boned
    chicken breast halves**
¼ teaspoon salt
¼ teaspoon garlic powder
**2 bunches fresh basil (about
    20 large basil leaves)**

Vegetable cooking spray
Tomato-Basil Pasta (facing page)
Garnish: fresh basil sprigs

Place chicken between two sheets of heavy-duty plastic wrap; flatten to ¼-
inch thickness, using a meat mallet or rolling pin.

Sprinkle chicken evenly with salt and garlic powder. Arrange basil leaves
in a single layer over chicken pieces. Starting at short ends, roll up 2 chicken

breasts. Place each roll on top of a remaining chicken breast, and roll up, forming two large rolls. Secure rolls with wooden picks.

Coat grill rack with cooking spray; place on grill over medium-hot coals (350° to 400°). Place chicken rolls on rack; grill, covered, 18 to 20 minutes or until chicken is done. Remove chicken rolls from grill; let stand 5 minutes. Cut each roll into thin slices.

To serve, place 1 cup Tomato-Basil Pasta on each of four individual serving plates; arrange chicken slices evenly over Tomato-Basil Pasta. Garnish, if desired. Yield: 4 servings.

Tomato-Basil Pasta

1 (8-ounce) package thin
    spaghetti, uncooked
1 tablespoon reduced-calorie
    margarine
2 cloves garlic, minced

1 cup peeled, seeded, and finely
    chopped tomato
¼ cup chopped fresh basil
¼ cup lemon juice
¼ cup dry white wine

Cook pasta according to package directions, omitting salt and fat; drain.

Melt margarine in a large saucepan over medium heat; add garlic, and cook, stirring constantly, 1 minute. Add pasta, tomato, and remaining ingredients; toss gently. Yield: 4 cups.

Cornish Hen with Chutney Glaze

1 (1¼-pound) Cornish hen,
    skinned
Vegetable cooking spray

2 tablespoons chopped mango
    chutney
2 teaspoons Dijon mustard

Per serving:
Calories 243 (30% from fat)
Fat 8.1g (sat 2.1g;
    mono 2.7g; poly 1.7g)
Cholesterol 91mg
Sodium 270mg
Carbohydrate 10.8g
Fiber 0.0g
Protein 29.7g

Remove and discard giblets from hen. Rinse hen thoroughly with cold water; pat dry with paper towels. Split hen in half lengthwise, using an electric knife.

Place hen halves, cut sides down, on a rack in a roasting pan coated with cooking spray. Combine chutney and mustard; brush one-third of chutney mixture over hen halves.

Bake, uncovered, at 325° for 50 to 55 minutes or until hen halves are done, basting twice with remaining chutney mixture. Yield: 2 servings.

Grilled Turkey Breast with Cranberry Salsa

☀ **Per serving:**
Calories 202 (14% from fat)
Fat 3.1g (sat 0.9g;
   mono 0.7g; poly 0.8g)
Cholesterol 58mg
Sodium 93mg
Carbohydrate 17.5g
Fiber 1.2g
Protein 25.6g

1 (6-pound) bone-in turkey breast
1 cup cranberry juice drink
¼ cup chopped fresh cilantro
¼ cup orange juice
¼ cup olive oil
1 teaspoon salt
1 teaspoon pepper
1 (12-ounce) package fresh or
   frozen cranberries
½ cup packed fresh cilantro
   leaves

½ cup coarsely chopped dried
   apricots
½ cup coarsely chopped purple
   onion
½ cup honey
2 tablespoons fresh lime juice
2 large oranges, peeled, seeded,
   and coarsely chopped
2 fresh jalapeño peppers, seeded
   and coarsely chopped
Vegetable cooking spray

Rinse turkey thoroughly with cold water; pat dry with paper towels. Remove and discard skin, bone, and tendons from turkey, separating breast halves; place turkey in a large heavy-duty, zip-top plastic bag.

Combine cranberry juice and next 5 ingredients in a jar; cover tightly, and shake vigorously. Reserve ½ cup juice mixture; cover and chill. Pour remaining juice mixture over turkey. Seal bag, and marinate in refrigerator 8 hours, turning bag occasionally.

Position knife blade in food processor bowl; add cranberries and next 7 ingredients. Pulse until chopped, stopping once to scrape down sides. (Do not overprocess.) Transfer mixture to a serving bowl; cover and chill.

Remove turkey from marinade, discarding marinade. Coat grill rack with cooking spray; place on grill over medium-hot coals (350° to 400°). Place turkey on rack; grill, covered, 20 minutes on each side or until a meat thermometer inserted into thickest part of breast registers 170°, basting occasionally with reserved ½ cup juice mixture.

Remove turkey from grill; let stand 10 minutes before slicing. Slice turkey, and serve with cranberry mixture. Yield: 16 servings.

Note: For best flavor and texture, buy a bone-in turkey breast, and have the butcher skin and bone it for you. Commercially boned turkey breasts are usually made from pressed and formed meat.

Roast Turkey Breast with Onion Gravy

*The oven cooking bag called for in this recipe ensures you'll get
a succulent, no-fuss turkey that folks will rave about.*

1 (5- to 5½-pound) bone-in
    turkey breast, skinned
2 stalks celery, halved
1 medium onion, peeled
Vegetable cooking spray
1½ tablespoons lemon-pepper
    seasoning
1½ teaspoons garlic powder
1½ teaspoons onion powder
1 teaspoon poultry seasoning

½ teaspoon paprika
3 tablespoons all-purpose flour,
    divided
3 tablespoons instant nonfat dry
    milk powder
½ teaspoon chicken-flavored
    bouillon granules
½ teaspoon browning-and-
    seasoning sauce
½ cup water

Per serving:
Calories 159 (11% from fat)
Fat 2.0g (sat 0.6g;
    mono 0.3g; poly 0.5g)
Cholesterol 70mg
Sodium 520mg
Carbohydrate 4.7g
Fiber 0.5g
Protein 28.7g

Rinse turkey thoroughly with cold water; pat dry with paper towels. Place celery and onion in breast cavity of turkey; coat turkey with cooking spray. Combine lemon-pepper seasoning and next 4 ingredients; sprinkle over turkey.

Shake 2 tablespoons flour in a large oven cooking bag; place bag in a large shallow roasting pan. Place turkey in bag; close bag, and seal. Bake turkey at 325° for 1½ hours.

Cut three ½-inch slits in top of bag, following package directions. Insert a meat thermometer through bag into thickest part of breast, making sure it does not touch bone. Bake turkey until meat thermometer registers 170° (about 1 hour).

Remove pan from oven; carefully cut a large slit in top of cooking bag. Remove turkey from bag, reserving 2 cups drippings for gravy. Remove celery and onion from breast cavity of turkey. Discard celery; reserve onion. Transfer turkey to a serving platter; let stand 10 to 15 minutes before carving.

Pour reserved drippings through a wire-mesh strainer into container of an electric blender; add reserved onion. Cover and process until smooth. Pour mixture into a small saucepan; stir in remaining 1 tablespoon flour, milk powder, and remaining 3 ingredients. Bring to a boil; reduce heat, and simmer 5 minutes, stirring often. Serve gravy with sliced turkey. Yield: 13 servings.

Stuffed Turkey Breast

☀ Per serving:
Calories 192 (15% from fat)
Fat 3.2g (sat 0.7g;
   mono 1.0g; poly 0.8g)
Cholesterol 70mg
Sodium 177mg
Carbohydrate 10.6g
Fiber 0.6g
Protein 28.9g

1 (5-pound) bone-in turkey breast
Vegetable cooking spray
½ cup diced onion
⅓ cup diced celery
2 cups cooked wild rice (cooked
   without salt or fat)
⅓ cup unsweetened applesauce
¼ cup chopped pecans, toasted
¼ cup currants
2 tablespoons minced fresh
   parsley

½ teaspoon salt
¼ teaspoon pepper
¼ teaspoon ground cinnamon
¼ teaspoon apple pie spice
¼ teaspoon poultry seasoning
¾ teaspoon cornstarch
¼ teaspoon apple pie spice
1 cup unsweetened apple juice

Rinse turkey thoroughly with cold water; pat dry with paper towels. Remove and discard skin, bone, and tendons from turkey, leaving breast halves connected. Trim any excess fat from turkey. Place turkey on a sheet of heavy-duty plastic wrap with inside of breast facing up.

Starting from center, slice horizontally through thickest portion of each side of breast to, but not through, outer edges. Flip cut pieces over to enlarge breast. Place heavy-duty plastic wrap over turkey, and pound to a more even thickness, using a meat mallet or rolling pin and placing loose pieces of turkey over thinner portions. Set turkey aside.

Coat a large nonstick skillet with cooking spray; place over medium-high heat until hot. Add onion and celery; cook, stirring constantly, until tender. Remove from heat; stir in rice and next 9 ingredients.

Spread rice mixture over turkey breast to within 1 inch of edges. Roll up turkey breast, jellyroll fashion, starting with short side. Tie securely at 2-inch intervals with heavy string. Place turkey roll, seam side down, on a rack in a roasting pan coated with cooking spray.

Combine cornstarch, ¼ teaspoon apple pie spice, and apple juice in a small saucepan. Bring to a boil over medium-high heat, stirring often; boil 1 minute. Brush apple juice mixture over turkey roll. Insert a meat thermometer into thickest portion of turkey roll.

Cover and bake at 325° for 1 hour and 20 minutes. Uncover and bake 1 hour and 10 minutes or until meat thermometer registers 170°, basting often with apple juice mixture.

Transfer turkey roll to a serving platter; let stand 15 minutes. Remove string, and cut roll into 13 slices. Yield: 13 servings.

Turkey Cutlets Parmesan

*You'll have an Italian-inspired classic on the table
in less than 30 minutes with this superquick entrée.
Sip a glass of dry red wine while the cutlets bake.*

1 large egg, lightly beaten
2 teaspoons vegetable oil
½ cup Italian-seasoned
   breadcrumbs
2 tablespoons grated Parmesan
   cheese

1 pound turkey breast cutlets
Vegetable cooking spray
½ cup low-fat marinara sauce or
   pasta sauce

Per serving:
Calories 273 (27% from fat)
Fat 8.1g (sat 2.2g;
   mono 1.7g; poly 1.8g)
Cholesterol 123mg
Sodium 678mg
Carbohydrate 15.2g
Fiber 0.6g
Protein 32.7g

Combine egg and oil in a shallow dish. Combine breadcrumbs and cheese in a shallow dish. Dip cutlets in egg mixture; dredge in breadcrumb mixture. Place cutlets on a baking sheet coated with cooking spray.

Coat cutlets lightly with cooking spray. Bake at 350° for 12 to 15 minutes or until done.

Place marinara sauce in a microwave-safe bowl. Cover and microwave at MEDIUM-HIGH (70% power) 2 minutes, stirring once. Spoon warm sauce over cutlets. Serve immediately. Yield: 4 servings.

Turkey Piccata

1 tablespoon lemon juice
½ pound turkey breast cutlets
1½ tablespoons all-purpose flour
½ teaspoon paprika
¼ teaspoon ground white pepper
½ teaspoon olive oil

¼ cup dry white wine
1 tablespoon lemon juice
1 tablespoon drained capers
1½ teaspoons chopped fresh
   parsley

Per serving:
Calories 189 (14% from fat)
Fat 3.0g (sat 0.7g;
   mono 1.2g; poly 0.6g)
Cholesterol 68mg
Sodium 520mg
Carbohydrate 6.6g
Fiber 0.3g
Protein 27.7g

Drizzle 1 tablespoon lemon juice over cutlets. Combine flour, paprika, and pepper; dredge cutlets in flour mixture.

Heat oil in a medium nonstick skillet over medium-high heat until hot. Add cutlets; cook 2 minutes on each side or until browned. Transfer cutlets to a serving platter; set aside, and keep warm.

Combine wine and 1 tablespoon lemon juice in skillet; bring to a boil over medium heat, stirring constantly. Add capers, and cook 1 minute. Pour caper mixture over cutlets, and sprinkle with parsley. Yield: 2 servings.

MEATLESS MAIN DISHES

*Y*ou're flipping through this cookbook, trying to find something for supper. Will it be burgers or chicken pot pie? Then you happen upon **Three-Bean Enchiladas**, and you decide on a meatless meal. Not just because it's healthy; it's also hearty and incredibly tasty. There's something satisfying about the way vegetables, beans, pastas, grains, cheeses, and spices create fabulous flavor explosions. Our best-kept secrets? Try **Baked Potatoes with Broccoli and Cheese, Veggie Soft Tacos,** and **Lentils and Rice Casserole**. They'll please even meat-and-potato lovers.

Spinach-Stuffed Shells (page 129)

Baked Potatoes with Broccoli and Cheese

Mother always told you to eat your vegetables. But she never told you how yummy vegetables could be when doused with a rich, velvety cheese sauce like this spud topper.

Per serving:
Calories 257 (12% from fat)
Fat 3.5g (sat 1.4g;
    mono 0.0g; poly 0.2g)
Cholesterol 8mg
Sodium 361mg
Carbohydrate 46.9g
Fiber 5.4g
Protein 12.8g

6 (8-ounce) baking potatoes
½ cup plain nonfat yogurt
3 tablespoons minced onion
⅛ teaspoon ground white pepper
5 cups chopped fresh broccoli
2½ tablespoons cornstarch
⅔ cup skim milk

⅔ cup canned reduced-sodium
    chicken broth, undiluted
4 ounces light process cheese
    spread, cubed
2 teaspoons reduced-calorie
    margarine
Paprika

Scrub potatoes; bake at 450° for 1 hour or until done. Cool slightly.

Cut a lengthwise strip (1½ inches wide) from top of each potato; discard strips. Scoop out pulp, leaving ¼-inch-thick shells; set shells aside.

Baked Potato with Broccoli and Cheese

DELIGHTFUL *Lites*

t at
ture
50°

eam

oth.
ntil
elts.
over
s.

d

r

ked

r

, and

Place
gar-
ext 4
, stir-

poon
rinkle
heese

melts. Yield: 4 servings.

Per serving:
Calories 454 (21% from fat)
Fat 10.8g (sat 5.1g;
   mono 2.7g; poly 1.1g)
Cholesterol 28mg
Sodium 643mg
Carbohydrate 61.9g
Fiber 9.3g
Protein 30.3g

Bean and Cornbread Casserole

This ingredient list might seem a little intimidating at first glance, but look again. You probably have most of the ingredients on hand, and you'll enjoy a 30-minute reprieve while this one-dish meal bakes.

Per serving:
Calories 396 (20% from fat)
Fat 9.0g (sat 2.7g;
    mono 2.5g; poly 3.0g)
Cholesterol 10mg
Sodium 502mg
Carbohydrate 61.8g
Fiber 5.9g
Protein 18.3g

Vegetable cooking spray
1 cup chopped onion
½ cup chopped green pepper
2 cloves garlic, minced
1 (16-ounce) can kidney beans, drained
1 (16-ounce) can pinto beans, drained
1 (16-ounce) can no-salt-added whole tomatoes, undrained and chopped
1 (8-ounce) can no-salt-added tomato sauce
1 teaspoon chili powder
½ teaspoon pepper
½ teaspoon prepared mustard

⅛ teaspoon hot sauce
1 cup yellow cornmeal
1 cup all-purpose flour
2½ teaspoons baking powder
½ teaspoon salt
1 tablespoon sugar
1¼ cups skim milk
½ cup egg substitute
3 tablespoons vegetable oil
1 (8½-ounce) can no-salt-added cream-style corn
1 cup (4 ounces) shredded reduced-fat sharp Cheddar cheese
Garnish: miniature hot peppers

Coat a large nonstick skillet with cooking spray; place over medium-high heat until hot. Add onion, green pepper, and garlic; cook, stirring constantly, until tender. Stir in kidney beans and next 7 ingredients; cover and cook 5 minutes, stirring occasionally. Pour bean mixture into a 13- x 9- x 2-inch baking dish coated with cooking spray. Set aside.

Combine cornmeal and next 4 ingredients in a large bowl. Combine milk and next 3 ingredients; add to cornmeal mixture, stirring until dry ingredients are moistened. Pour batter evenly over bean mixture. Bake, uncovered, at 375° for 30 minutes or until cornbread is done. Remove casserole from oven, and sprinkle with cheese; cover and let stand 5 minutes or until cheese melts. Cut into squares to serve. Garnish, if desired. Yield: 8 servings.

Bean and Cornbread Casserole (facing page)

Vegetable Burritos

Vegetable cooking spray
1 teaspoon olive oil
2 cups sliced fresh mushrooms
½ cup chopped onion
½ cup chopped green pepper
1 clove garlic, pressed
¾ cup drained canned kidney
    beans
1 tablespoon chopped ripe olives

⅛ teaspoon pepper
4 (8-inch) fat-free flour tortillas
¼ cup nonfat sour cream
¾ cup no-salt-added salsa,
    divided
½ cup (2 ounces) shredded
    reduced-fat sharp Cheddar
    cheese

Per serving:
Calories 256 (18% from fat)
Fat 5.0g (sat 1.9g;
   mono 1.8g; poly 0.4g)
Cholesterol 10mg
Sodium 648mg
Carbohydrate 40.4g
Fiber 3.4g
Protein 12.9g

Coat a large nonstick skillet with cooking spray; add oil. Place over medium-high heat until hot. Add mushrooms and next 3 ingredients; cook, stirring constantly, until tender. Drain mixture, and return to skillet; stir in beans, olives, and ⅛ teaspoon pepper.

Spoon one-fourth of bean mixture down center of each tortilla. Top each with 1 tablespoon sour cream, 1 tablespoon salsa, and 2 tablespoons cheese; fold opposite sides over filling.

Coat skillet with cooking spray; place over medium-high heat until hot. Place burritos, seam sides down, in skillet; cook 1 minute on each side or until lightly browned. Serve burritos with remaining ½ cup salsa. Yield: 4 servings.

Easy Cheesy Manicotti

Take the easy way when it comes to stuffing manicotti shells.
First, fill a heavy-duty, zip-top plastic bag with the cheese mixture.
Then seal the bag, and snip a large corner from the bottom. Finally,
just squeeze the bag to pipe the cheese mixture into the shells.

½ cup freshly grated Parmesan cheese, divided
2 cups 1% low-fat cottage cheese
½ cup part-skim ricotta cheese
2 tablespoons chopped fresh parsley
½ teaspoon dried Italian seasoning
¼ teaspoon garlic powder
1 egg, lightly beaten
12 cooked manicotti shells (cooked without salt or fat)
1 (15½-ounce) jar no-salt-added spaghetti sauce

Combine ⅓ cup Parmesan cheese, cottage cheese, and next 5 ingredients; stuff each shell with ¼ cup cheese mixture. Arrange shells in a 13- x 9- x 2-inch baking dish. Pour spaghetti sauce over shells. Cover and bake at 375° for 25 minutes or until heated. Sprinkle with remaining Parmesan cheese before serving. Yield: 6 servings.

Pasta with Peanut Sauce

You'll discover a mélange of typical Thai flavors in this quick-to-fix recipe.

8 ounces spaghetti, uncooked
3 medium-size yellow squash
1 medium-size sweet red pepper
6 green onions, cut into 2-inch pieces
1 tablespoon dark sesame oil
1 tablespoon minced garlic
¼ cup reduced-fat creamy peanut spread
¼ cup low-sodium soy sauce
3 tablespoons fresh lime juice
1 tablespoon sugar
1 teaspoon dried crushed red pepper

Cook spaghetti according to package directions, omitting salt and fat. Drain.
    Cut squash in half lengthwise; cut halves into slices. Seed sweet red pepper, and cut into thin strips. Cook squash, sweet red pepper, and green onions in a saucepan in boiling water to cover 1 to 2 minutes or until crisp-tender. Drain vegetables, and set aside.

Heat oil in a large nonstick skillet over medium heat until hot. Add garlic; cook, stirring constantly, 1 minute. Add peanut spread, stirring until smooth. Stir in soy sauce and remaining 3 ingredients.

Add vegetable mixture to skillet, tossing gently to coat. Remove vegetable mixture from skillet with a slotted spoon. Add cooked spaghetti to sauce in skillet, tossing to coat. Transfer spaghetti to a serving plate, and top with vegetable mixture. Serve immediately. Yield: 4 (1¼-cup) servings.

Spinach-Stuffed Shells

The smidgen of brown sugar in this recipe plays an important role. It adds a hint of sweetness and enhances the flavor of the sauce. You'll find these scintillating shells pictured on page 112.

24 jumbo macaroni shells, uncooked
Vegetable cooking spray
1 small onion, diced
2 (14½-ounce) cans no-salt-added whole tomatoes, undrained and chopped
1 (8-ounce) can no-salt-added tomato sauce
1 (6-ounce) can no-salt-added tomato paste
2 teaspoons brown sugar

1 teaspoon dried oregano
½ teaspoon salt
¼ teaspoon pepper
2 (10-ounce) packages frozen chopped spinach, thawed
2 cups 1% low-fat cottage cheese
1 cup (4 ounces) shredded part-skim mozzarella cheese
¼ teaspoon pepper
½ cup freshly grated Parmesan cheese
Garnish: fresh oregano sprigs

Per serving:
Calories 278 (18% from fat)
Fat 5.5g (sat 3.0g; mono 1.4g; poly 0.2g)
Cholesterol 15mg
Sodium 639mg
Carbohydrate 37.4g
Fiber 4.0g
Protein 20.4g

Cook shells according to package directions, omitting salt and fat. Drain.

Coat a large nonstick skillet with cooking spray; place over medium-high heat until hot. Add onion, and cook, stirring constantly, until tender. Stir in tomato and next 6 ingredients; bring to a boil. Cover, reduce heat, and simmer 20 minutes, stirring occasionally.

Drain spinach, pressing between layers of paper towels to remove excess moisture. Combine spinach, cottage cheese, mozzarella cheese, and ¼ teaspoon pepper; stuff each shell with 2 tablespoons spinach mixture.

Spread 2 cups tomato mixture in a 13- x 9- x 2-inch baking dish coated with cooking spray. Arrange shells in dish; top with remaining tomato mixture. Cover and bake at 350° for 35 minutes or until heated. Sprinkle each serving with 1 tablespoon Parmesan cheese. Garnish, if desired. Yield: 8 servings.

SALADS

*R*emember when salad was a wedge of iceberg lettuce dolloped with dressing? Today, countless varieties of leafy greens, aromatic herbs, and unique vegetables and fruits ensure that salads tease you with compelling textures, colors, and flavors. And this chapter does the same. Here are some hints: To savor summertime freshness, spoon up Basil-Tomato Couscous Salad. It's great as a side salad or main dish. For something cool, crisp, and slightly sweet, try Cabbage-Pineapple Slaw. And when hunger really hits, go for Chicken Taco Salad—our favorite.

Fruited Greens with Orange Vinaigrette (page 132)

Hearts of Romaine with Caper Vinaigrette

*Tender romaine leaves fan each salad plate as
a base for this simple but elegant salad. Sherry and sugar
balance the saltiness of capers in the vinaigrette.*

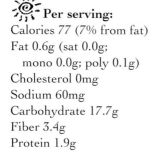 **Per serving:**
Calories 41 (22% from fat)
Fat 1.0g (sat 0.1g;
    mono 0.6g; poly 0.2g)
Cholesterol 0mg
Sodium 371mg
Carbohydrate 5.6g
Fiber 2.0g
Protein 1.9g

½ cup water
3 tablespoons rice vinegar
1 tablespoon low-sodium soy
    sauce
1 tablespoon sherry
1 teaspoon sugar
1 teaspoon cornstarch
1 teaspoon olive oil

¼ teaspoon minced garlic
2 tablespoons drained capers
1 (12-ounce) package romaine
    lettuce hearts
¾ cup sliced cucumber
3 slices purple onion, separated
    into rings

Combine first 8 ingredients in a small saucepan; bring to a boil, stirring constantly. Boil 1 minute. Remove from heat, and stir in capers. Cover and chill.

Trim ends of romaine hearts; discard ends. Separate hearts into individual leaves. Arrange leaves evenly on six salad plates. Arrange cucumber and onion evenly over lettuce. Drizzle evenly with caper mixture. Yield: 6 servings.

Fruited Greens with Orange Vinaigrette

Per serving:
Calories 77 (7% from fat)
Fat 0.6g (sat 0.0g;
    mono 0.0g; poly 0.1g)
Cholesterol 0mg
Sodium 60mg
Carbohydrate 17.7g
Fiber 3.4g
Protein 1.9g

5 small oranges
1 tablespoon honey
2 teaspoons sherry vinegar
2 teaspoons coarse-grained
    mustard

1½ cups loosely packed
    watercress leaves
1½ cups arugula
1 cup thinly sliced Belgian endive
2 cups fresh strawberries, sliced

Grate 1 teaspoon rind from oranges; set grated rind aside. Peel and section 3 oranges; set sections aside. Squeeze enough juice from remaining 2 oranges to measure ½ cup juice. Combine juice and honey in a small saucepan; bring to a boil. Reduce heat, and simmer, uncovered, 8 minutes or until mixture is reduced to ⅓ cup, stirring occasionally. Cool.

Combine cooled juice mixture, grated orange rind, vinegar, and mustard in a jar. Cover tightly, and shake vigorously.

Combine watercress, arugula, and endive in a salad bowl; add juice mixture, and toss gently to coat. Arrange greens mixture evenly on four salad plates; top with orange sections and strawberry slices. Yield: 4 servings.

Spinach-Kiwifruit Salad

3 tablespoons water
2 tablespoons rice vinegar
2 teaspoons honey
1 teaspoon prepared mustard
1 teaspoon vegetable oil
½ teaspoon lemon juice

⅛ teaspoon onion powder
8 fresh spinach leaves
8 Boston lettuce leaves
2 kiwifruit, peeled and sliced
Garnish: lemon rind curls

 **Per serving:**
Calories 93 (28% from fat)
Fat 2.9g (sat 0.5g;
    mono 0.9g; poly 1.2g)
Cholesterol 0mg
Sodium 49mg
Carbohydrate 15.4g
Fiber 3.2g
Protein 1.8g

Combine first 7 ingredients in a jar. Cover tightly, and shake vigorously. Chill.

Arrange spinach and lettuce evenly on two salad plates; top evenly with kiwifruit. Garnish, if desired. Serve with dressing mixture. Yield: 2 servings.

Crimson Greens

In this salad, ruby raspberry vinaigrette blankets light and dark greens flecked with orange sections and sliced almonds.

1 cup water
¾ cup fresh raspberries
3 tablespoons sugar
1 tablespoon cornstarch
2 tablespoons lemon juice
2 tablespoons rice vinegar
2 tablespoons dry white wine
1 tablespoon vegetable oil

5 cups loosely packed Boston
    lettuce leaves (about
    ½ pound)
3 cups loosely packed watercress
    sprigs
2 cups fresh orange sections
1 tablespoon plus 1 teaspoon
    sliced almonds, toasted

Per serving:
Calories 111 (26% from fat)
Fat 3.2g (sat 0.5g;
    mono 1.1g; poly 1.3g)
Cholesterol 0mg
Sodium 8mg
Carbohydrate 19.9g
Fiber 5.2g
Protein 1.9g

Combine first 8 ingredients in a small saucepan. Bring mixture to a boil over medium-high heat, stirring constantly; boil 1 minute. Pour mixture through a wire-mesh strainer into a small bowl or jar, pressing mixture against sides of strainer with back of spoon; discard seeds and pulp. Cover and chill.

Arrange lettuce leaves evenly on six salad plates; arrange watercress sprigs and orange sections evenly over lettuce. Drizzle ¼ cup raspberry mixture over each salad; sprinkle evenly with almonds. Yield: 6 servings.

Carrot-Pineapple Salad

Colorful bits of pineapple, carrot, and golden raisins
float throughout this tangy-sweet gelatin salad.

1 (¼-ounce) envelope unflavored
  gelatin
1 cup cold water
1 (6-ounce) can frozen orange
  juice concentrate, thawed and
  undiluted
½ teaspoon grated orange rind

1 cup finely shredded carrot
½ cup golden raisins
1 (8-ounce) can unsweetened
  crushed pineapple, undrained
Vegetable cooking spray
7 green leaf lettuce leaves

Sprinkle gelatin over cold water in a small saucepan; let stand 1 minute. Cook over low heat, stirring until gelatin dissolves, about 2 minutes. Stir in orange juice concentrate and rind. Chill until the consistency of unbeaten egg white.

Fold carrot, raisins, and pineapple into gelatin mixture. Spoon mixture evenly into seven ½-cup molds coated with cooking spray. Cover and chill until firm. Unmold onto individual lettuce-lined salad plates. Yield: 7 servings.

Frozen Strawberry Salad

Stash this fruit-studded cream cheese mixture in the freezer,
and you won't have to fret about making a salad for supper.
You'll have about a month to serve 12 frosty salads.

1 (8-ounce) carton light
  process cream cheese,
  softened
½ cup sugar
2 medium bananas, sliced
1 (15¼-ounce) can unsweetened
  crushed pineapple, undrained

1 (8-ounce) container frozen
  reduced-calorie whipped
  topping, thawed
2 cups frozen unsweetened
  whole strawberries, thawed
  and halved
Garnish: fresh strawberry fans

Beat cream cheese at medium speed of an electric mixer until creamy. Gradually add sugar; beat until smooth. Fold in banana and next 3 ingredients. Spoon mixture into a 13- x 9- x 2-inch dish; cover salad, and freeze until firm.

Remove salad from freezer; let stand 10 minutes. Cut into squares. Cover and freeze any remaining salad. Garnish, if desired. Yield: 12 servings.

Melon Balls with Creamy Mint Dressing

*A cool, creamy dressing laced with mint crowns
a colorful rainbow of melon balls in this summery salad.*

1½ cups watermelon balls
1½ cups cantaloupe balls
1 cup honeydew melon balls
1 cup fresh pineapple chunks

1 cup julienne-sliced jicama
6 green leaf lettuce leaves
Creamy Mint Dressing

Combine first 5 ingredients; spoon evenly into six individual lettuce-lined bowls. Drizzle evenly with Creamy Mint Dressing. Yield: 6 servings.

Creamy Mint Dressing

½ cup plain low-fat yogurt
⅓ cup diced cucumber
3 tablespoons reduced-calorie
  mayonnaise

2 teaspoons minced fresh mint
⅛ teaspoon celery seeds
⅛ teaspoon ground white pepper

Combine all ingredients; cover and chill. Yield: ¾ cup.

Per serving:
Calories 106 (23% from fat)
Fat 2.7g (sat 0.9g;
   mono 0.1g, poly 0.1g)
Cholesterol 4mg
Sodium 81mg
Carbohydrate 19.3g
Fiber 1.7g
Protein 2.3g

Sesame Waldorf Salad

*Here's Waldorf salad with a couple of twists—orange
low-fat yogurt binds the salad and adds creamy sweetness,
while toasted sesame seeds contribute nutty crunch.*

1 cup chopped Red Delicious
  apple
1 cup seedless green grape halves

1 cup sliced celery
⅓ cup orange low-fat yogurt
2 teaspoons sesame seeds, toasted

Combine first 4 ingredients; toss gently. Sprinkle with sesame seeds, and serve immediately. Yield: 4 (¾-cup) servings.

Per serving:
Calories 85 (15% from fat)
Fat 1.4g (sat 0.4g;
   mono 0.4g; poly 0.5g)
Cholesterol 1mg
Sodium 37mg
Carbohydrate 18.4g
Fiber 2.4g
Protein 1.7g

Cabbage-Pineapple Slaw

Cabbage-Pineapple Slaw

We decided that someone at a covered-dish dinner mixed Waldorf salad with coleslaw and created this clever combo.

☀ **Per serving:**
Calories 108 (29% from fat)
Fat 3.5g (sat 0.3g;
    mono 0.0g; poly 0.1g)
Cholesterol 4mg
Sodium 109mg
Carbohydrate 20.2g
Fiber 2.9g
Protein 1.2g

1 (8-ounce) can pineapple tidbits
    in juice, undrained
3 cups finely shredded cabbage
1½ cups chopped Red Delicious
    apple
½ cup chopped celery

¼ cup golden raisins
¼ cup reduced-calorie
    mayonnaise
Cabbage leaves (optional)
Garnish: Red Delicious apple
    slices

Drain pineapple, reserving 3 tablespoons juice. Combine drained pineapple, shredded cabbage, and next 3 ingredients in a large bowl.

Combine reserved pineapple juice and mayonnaise; add to cabbage mixture, tossing gently. Spoon mixture into a cabbage leaf-lined bowl, if desired. Cover and chill. Garnish, if desired. Yield: 5 (1-cup) servings.

Black Bean Salad

This salad is extremely accommodating. It's ready when you are because it's made ahead. And you can spoon it up as either a side dish or a main dish.

1¼ cups chopped tomato
¾ cup chopped sweet red pepper
⅔ cup sliced green onions
½ cup chopped celery
2 tablespoons chopped fresh
    cilantro leaves
1 tablespoon grated lemon rind
2 (15-ounce) cans black beans,
    drained

1 clove garlic, minced
¾ cup water
1 tablespoon olive oil
¼ teaspoon ground red pepper
1 (0.7-ounce) envelope Italian
    salad dressing mix

Per serving:
Calories 136 (18% from fat)
Fat 2.7g (sat 0.4g;
    mono 1.5g; poly 0.5g)
Cholesterol 0mg
Sodium 569mg
Carbohydrate 22.6g
Fiber 4.4g
Protein 7.0g

Combine first 8 ingredients in a large bowl; set aside.

Combine water and remaining 3 ingredients in a jar. Cover tightly, and shake vigorously. Pour dressing mixture over bean mixture, and toss gently. Cover and chill. Toss gently before serving. Yield: 7 (¾-cup) servings.

Green Beans with Tarragon Dressing

1½ pounds fresh green beans
1 cup nonfat mayonnaise
⅓ cup chopped fresh parsley
¼ cup chopped onion
¼ cup 1% low-fat cottage cheese
3 tablespoons tarragon
    vinegar

2 tablespoons skim milk
1½ teaspoons lemon juice
½ teaspoon anchovy paste
4 heads Belgian endive, sliced
    crosswise

Per serving:
Calories 68 (4% from fat)
Fat 0.3g (sat 0.1g;
    mono 0.0g; poly 0.1g)
Cholesterol 0mg
Sodium 465mg
Carbohydrate 14.7g
Fiber 1.8g
Protein 3.3g

Wash beans; remove strings, and trim ends. Arrange beans in a steamer basket over boiling water. Cover and steam 12 minutes or until crisp-tender. Drain beans; plunge into ice water, and drain. Cover and chill.

Position knife blade in food processor bowl; add mayonnaise and next 7 ingredients. Process 1 minute or until mixture is smooth, stopping once to scrape down sides. Transfer mixture to a small bowl; cover and chill at least 1 hour.

Arrange endive evenly on eight individual salad plates; top evenly with beans. Drizzle evenly with mayonnaise mixture. Yield: 8 servings.

Company Salad with Wine Vinaigrette

Make extra dressing to keep on hand in the refrigerator.
This versatile vinaigrette's light, fresh taste (it contains only
a smidgen of oil) scored winning points with our staff.

40 small fresh green beans or
 snow pea pods
20 Bibb lettuce leaves, torn
4 large mushrooms, sliced
1 head Belgian endive, sliced
 crosswise

1 large tomato, thinly sliced
1 (14.4-ounce) can hearts of palm,
 drained and sliced crosswise
Wine Vinaigrette

Wash green beans; remove strings, and trim ends. Cook beans in boiling water to cover 30 seconds; drain and plunge into ice water until chilled. Remove beans from water; drain on paper towels.

Combine green beans, torn lettuce, and next 4 ingredients in a large bowl, and toss gently to combine. Spoon bean mixture evenly onto four individual salad plates; drizzle salads evenly with Wine Vinaigrette. Yield: 4 servings.

Wine Vinaigrette

½ cup chopped green onions
½ cup red wine vinegar
1 teaspoon dried parsley flakes
1 teaspoon vegetable oil

½ teaspoon sugar
¼ teaspoon salt
¼ teaspoon pepper

Combine all ingredients in container of an electric blender; cover and process 30 seconds. Yield: ⅔ cup.

Marinated Tomato Slices

Marinated Tomato Slices

Thick slices of red and yellow tomatoes add bold color to this simple salad.

4 large red or yellow tomatoes, cut into ¼-inch slices
¼ cup lemon juice
2 tablespoons minced purple onion
2 tablespoons red wine vinegar
1 tablespoon chopped fresh basil or 1 teaspoon dried basil

¼ teaspoon freshly ground pepper
1 clove garlic, minced
Green leaf lettuce leaves (optional)

Per serving:
Calories 25 (11% from fat)
Fat 0.3g (sat 0.0g; mono 0.1g; poly 0.1g)
Cholesterol 0mg
Sodium 9mg
Carbohydrate 5.9g
Fiber 1.4g
Protein 1.0g

Arrange tomato slices in a large shallow dish. Combine lemon juice and next 5 ingredients; pour over tomato slices, turning to coat. Cover and marinate in refrigerator at least 2 hours.

Arrange tomato slices evenly on eight individual lettuce-lined salad plates, if desired. Spoon marinade evenly over tomato slices. Yield: 8 servings.

Grilled Chicken Salad with Mango Salsa

Mango salsa and raspberry dressing team up to make one kicky chicken salad. Keep extra dressing on hand to drizzle over a green salad for a refreshing change from Ranch or Italian dressing.

4 (4-ounce) skinned and boned
   chicken breast halves
½ cup plus 1 tablespoon Raspberry Dressing, divided

Vegetable cooking spray
8 cups mixed baby salad greens
Mango Salsa

Place chicken in a large heavy-duty, zip-top plastic bag; add ¼ cup Raspberry Dressing. Seal bag; marinate in refrigerator 2 hours, turning bag occasionally. Cover and chill remaining Raspberry Dressing.

Remove chicken from marinade; discard marinade. Coat grill rack with cooking spray; place on grill over medium-hot coals (350° to 400°). Place chicken on rack; grill, covered, 5 minutes on each side or until done. Remove from grill; let stand 5 minutes. Cut chicken into thin strips.

Combine salad greens and remaining ¼ cup plus 1 tablespoon Raspberry Dressing, tossing to coat. Arrange greens mixture evenly on four individual serving plates; top evenly with chicken and Mango Salsa. Yield: 4 servings.

Raspberry Dressing

¼ cup plus 2 tablespoons lime
   juice
¼ cup seedless red raspberry jam
3 tablespoons hot red pepper jelly
1 tablespoon vegetable oil

½ teaspoon dry mustard
¼ teaspoon salt
¼ teaspoon freshly ground
   pepper
1 large clove garlic, halved

Combine all ingredients in container of an electric blender; cover and process until smooth. Cover and chill. Yield: ¾ cup.

Mango Salsa

4 medium mangoes, peeled and
   finely chopped
¼ cup chopped fresh basil
3 tablespoons Raspberry
   Dressing

1 green jalapeño pepper, seeded
   and finely chopped
1 red jalapeño pepper, seeded and
   finely chopped

Combine all ingredients. Cover and chill. Yield: 2¼ cups.

Grilled Chicken Salad with Mango Salsa (facing page)

Chicken Pasta Salad

3 (4-ounce) skinned and boned
    chicken breast halves
3½ cups cooked small pasta shells
    (cooked without salt or fat)
3 cups fresh broccoli flowerets
1 cup sweet red pepper strips
¼ cup sliced green onions
6 ounces fresh snow pea pods,
    trimmed

¼ cup plus 1 tablespoon red wine
    vinegar
3 tablespoons vegetable oil
2 tablespoons honey
2 teaspoons sesame seeds, toasted
1 teaspoon hot sauce
½ teaspoon salt
½ teaspoon ground ginger
3 cloves garlic, minced

Per serving:
Calories 381 (27% from fat)
Fat 11.5g (sat 2.1g;
    mono 3.2g; poly 4.7g)
Cholesterol 39mg
Sodium 289mg
Carbohydrate 46.4g
Fiber 2.6g
Protein 22.3g

Place chicken in a medium saucepan; add water to cover. Bring to a boil; reduce heat to medium, and cook, uncovered, 15 minutes or until done. Drain; cool chicken slightly. Cut chicken into bite-size pieces.

    Combine chicken and pasta in a large bowl; add broccoli and next 3 ingredients, tossing gently. Combine vinegar and remaining 7 ingredients in a jar; cover tightly, and shake vigorously. Pour dressing mixture over chicken mixture; toss gently. Cover and chill 2 hours. Yield: 5 (2-cup) servings.

Chicken Taco Salad

Chicken Taco Salad

*A homemade seasoning mix spices up this south-of-the-border salad
served in shapely flour tortilla shells. We think your family will savor
the fiesta of flavors and praise this recipe as highly as we did.*

4 (4-ounce) skinned and boned
    chicken breast halves
2 tablespoons Tex-Mex Spice
    Mix, divided
Vegetable cooking spray
½ cup chopped green pepper
½ cup chopped sweet red pepper
½ cup chopped jicama
1 tablespoon chopped fresh
    cilantro

1 medium mango, peeled and
    chopped
2 tablespoons water
2 tablespoons lime juice
1 tablespoon vegetable oil
1 teaspoon sugar
4 (10-inch) flour tortillas
6 cups shredded Bibb lettuce
Lime slices (optional)

Coat chicken evenly with 1 tablespoon Tex-Mex Spice Mix. Cover chicken,
and chill 8 hours.

Coat a large nonstick skillet with cooking spray; place over medium heat. Add chicken, and cook 4 to 5 minutes on each side or until done. Remove chicken from skillet; cool. Chop chicken; cover and chill.

Combine chopped chicken, green pepper, and next 4 ingredients. Combine remaining 1 tablespoon Tex-Mex Spice Mix, water, and next 3 ingredients; drizzle over chicken mixture, and toss well. Set aside.

For each tortilla bowl, press 1 tortilla into a medium microwave-safe bowl; microwave each at HIGH 1½ minutes or until crisp. Set aside, and cool.

Arrange lettuce evenly in tortilla bowls; spoon chicken mixture evenly over lettuce. Serve with lime slices, if desired. Yield: 4 servings.

Tex-Mex Spice Mix

3 tablespoons chili powder	1 tablespoon black pepper
2 tablespoons ground cumin	1½ teaspoons ground red
1 tablespoon garlic powder	pepper
1 tablespoon salt	

Combine all ingredients. Store mixture in an airtight container in a cool, dark, dry place up to 3 months. Use to season chicken or beef. Yield: ½ cup.

Turkey Waldorf Salad with Yogurt Dressing

1 cup chopped cooked turkey	½ cup plain low-fat yogurt
1 cup diced Red Delicious apple	1 tablespoon honey
½ cup chopped celery	1 teaspoon grated orange rind
2 tablespoons chopped walnuts	4 green leaf lettuce leaves
2 tablespoons raisins	

Combine first 5 ingredients in a medium bowl. Combine yogurt, honey, and orange rind; pour over turkey mixture, and toss gently.

Arrange lettuce leaves evenly on two individual serving plates; top evenly with turkey mixture. Serve immediately. Yield: 2 servings.

Per serving:
Calories 306 (21% from fat)
Fat 7.0g (sat 1.1g;
  mono 1.4g; poly 3.6g)
Cholesterol 47mg
Sodium 122mg
Carbohydrate 36.7g
Fiber 3.8g
Protein 26.2g

SOUPS

*S*oup can warm you up or cool you down. It can balance the meal or *be* the meal. And just a few simple additions can turn it into rustic stew, chili, chowder, or gumbo. See how versatile soup can be with Tropical Gazpacho. Serve this chilled fruit soup as a first course or as a light dessert. Or entice your family with the heady aroma of French Onion Soup. Folks will think you spent all afternoon in the kitchen when you ladle up bowlfuls of Potato-Corn Chowder. But you can curl up with a good book instead—this soup's on in about 30 minutes!

Burgundy Beef Stew (page 161)

French Market Soup

1 (16-ounce) package dried bean soup mix (without seasoning packet)
10 cups water
1 cup cubed lean cooked ham
2 (16-ounce) cans no-salt-added whole tomatoes, undrained and chopped

1½ cups chopped onion
1 cup chopped celery
3 tablespoons lemon juice
1 teaspoon hot sauce
3 large cloves garlic, minced
¾ teaspoon salt
½ teaspoon pepper

Sort and wash beans; place in a Dutch oven. Cover with water 2 inches above beans. Bring to a boil; cover, remove from heat, and let stand 1 hour.

Drain beans, and return to Dutch oven; add 10 cups water and ham. Bring to a boil; cover, reduce heat, and simmer 1 hour or until beans are tender.

Add tomato and next 5 ingredients to Dutch oven; bring mixture to a boil. Reduce heat, and simmer, uncovered, 1 hour, stirring occasionally. Stir in salt and pepper. Yield: 8 (1½-cup) servings.

Chunky Chicken Noodle Soup

Our chicken soup may not cure the common cold, but it will comfort you with down-home goodness. Tender chunks of chicken and lots of curly noodles swim in a well-seasoned broth that will warm you to your toes.

1 (3-pound) broiler-fryer, skinned
4 cups water
¾ teaspoon poultry seasoning
¼ teaspoon dried thyme
3 celery tops
2 cups water
1 cup medium egg noodles, uncooked
½ cup sliced celery
½ cup sliced carrot

⅓ cup sliced green onions
2 tablespoons minced fresh parsley
2 teaspoons chicken-flavored bouillon granules
¼ teaspoon coarsely ground pepper
1 bay leaf
Additional coarsely ground pepper (optional)

Combine first 5 ingredients in a Dutch oven; bring to a boil. Cover, reduce heat, and simmer 45 minutes or until chicken is tender. Remove chicken from broth, reserving broth; set chicken aside to cool. Remove and discard celery tops from broth.

Skim fat from broth. Add 2 cups water and next 8 ingredients to broth; bring to a boil. Cover, reduce heat, and simmer 20 minutes.

Bone and coarsely chop chicken; add to broth mixture. Cook 5 minutes or until mixture is thoroughly heated. Remove and discard bay leaf. Ladle soup into individual bowls, and sprinkle with additional coarsely ground pepper, if desired. Yield: 6 (1-cup) servings.

Chunky Chicken Noodle Soup

Potato-Corn Chowder

You can bet the folks on our foods staff will be stirring up this chunky vegetable chowder in their own kitchens this winter. They lined up to make copies of the recipe after taste testing.

Per serving:
Calories 167 (5% from fat)
Fat 0.9g (sat 0.2g;
    mono 0.2g; poly 0.3g)
Cholesterol 2mg
Sodium 841mg
Carbohydrate 33.5g
Fiber 2.6g
Protein 8.4g

Vegetable cooking spray
¾ cup chopped green pepper
⅓ cup chopped onion
2¾ cups canned reduced-sodium chicken broth, undiluted
2 cups chopped red potato

1 teaspoon salt
¼ teaspoon pepper
¼ cup cornstarch
2¼ cups skim milk
2¼ cups frozen whole kernel corn
1 (2-ounce) jar diced pimiento

Coat a medium saucepan with cooking spray; place over medium-high heat until hot. Add chopped green pepper and onion; cook, stirring constantly, 5 minutes or until tender. Stir in broth and next 3 ingredients. Bring to a boil; reduce heat, and simmer, uncovered, 6 to 8 minutes or until potato is tender.

Combine cornstarch and skim milk, stirring until smooth; gradually add to potato mixture, stirring constantly. Stir in corn and pimiento; bring to a boil over medium heat, stirring constantly. Cook, stirring constantly, 1 minute or until mixture is thickened. Serve immediately. Yield: 5 (1½-cup) servings.

Potato-Corn Chowder

Chicken-Sausage Gumbo

¾ cup all-purpose flour
Vegetable cooking spray
6 (6-ounce) skinned chicken
    breast halves
1 cup chopped onion
½ cup chopped green pepper
½ cup sliced celery
2 quarts hot water
1 tablespoon low-sodium
    Worcestershire sauce
2 teaspoons reduced-sodium
    Cajun seasoning

1 teaspoon hot sauce
½ teaspoon dried thyme
¼ teaspoon salt
3 cloves garlic, minced
2 bay leaves
½ pound 80% fat-free smoked
    sausage, cut into ¼-inch slices
½ cup sliced green onions
5½ cups cooked long-grain rice
    (cooked without salt or fat)

Per serving:
Calories 253 (9% from fat)
Fat 2.4g (sat 0.7g;
   mono 0.6g; poly 0.4g)
Cholesterol 47mg
Sodium 307mg
Carbohydrate 49.8g
Fiber 1.2g
Protein 20.5g

Place flour in a 13- x 9- x 2-inch pan. Bake at 400° for 25 minutes or until flour is caramel colored, stirring every 5 minutes.

Coat a Dutch oven with cooking spray; place over medium-high heat until hot. Add chicken; cook 2 minutes on each side or until lightly browned. Drain on paper towels. Wipe drippings from Dutch oven with a paper towel.

Coat Dutch oven with cooking spray; place over medium-high heat. Add chopped onion, green pepper, and celery; cook, stirring constantly, until vegetables are tender. Sprinkle browned flour over vegetable mixture. Gradually stir in hot water; bring to a boil.

Add chicken, Worcestershire sauce, and next 6 ingredients to Dutch oven; cover, reduce heat, and simmer 1 hour. Remove chicken from Dutch oven; cool.

Brown sausage in a large nonstick skillet coated with cooking spray; drain and pat dry with paper towels. Add sausage to gumbo mixture in Dutch oven; cook, uncovered, 30 minutes, stirring occasionally. Stir in green onions; cook, uncovered, 30 additional minutes.

Bone chicken, and cut into strips. Add chicken strips to gumbo mixture; cook until thoroughly heated. Remove and discard bay leaves.

Spoon ½ cup rice into each of 11 individual bowls; top each serving with 1 cup gumbo. Yield: 11 servings.

SANDWICHES

If the brown bag blues have got you down, then you've come to the right place. Our savvy sandwiches will pick up the pace of any meal. If you're on the go, grab a Fajita in a Pita and head out the door. The pita pocket holds the filling, so nothing's left in your lap but a clean napkin. Gear up for the day with open-face Breakfast Sandwiches. They showcase tasty toppings too pretty to hide beneath slices of bread. And toast our slew of fun ways to slather on versatile sandwich spreads.

Fiesta Burgers (page 173)

SIDE DISHES

*W*e love side dishes, especially those with some pizzazz thrown in for good measure, like broccoli tossed with crushed red pepper and garlic, or noodles bathed in a fresh tomato-basil sauce. We'll tell you our chapter favorites right up front — Garlic and Lemon Linguine, Spicy Mexican Rice, and Southern-Style Creamed Corn. But don't let Orange-Spiced Carrots or Dried Apple Side Dish slip by untried, either. Whatever the main course, you'll find a just-right accompaniment within these pages.

Pasta Provençal (page 200)

185

Southern-Style Creamed Corn

Southern-Style Creamed Corn

*Thick slices of onion simmered with milky kernels of corn
give this creamy side dish it's fresh-from-the-farm taste.*

Per serving:
Calories 188 (12% from fat)
Fat 2.6g (sat 0.8g;
    mono 0.8g; poly 0.8g)
Cholesterol 3mg
Sodium 259mg
Carbohydrate 39.8g
Fiber 5.1g
Protein 7.0g

6 ears fresh corn
1 cup 1% low-fat milk, divided
2 teaspoons cornstarch

2 (½-inch-thick) onion slices
¼ teaspoon salt
¼ teaspoon pepper

Remove and discard husks and silks from corn. Cut corn from cobs, scraping
cobs well to remove all milk. Set corn aside.

Combine ¼ cup milk and cornstarch; set aside. Combine remaining ¾
cup milk and onion in a large saucepan; bring to a boil over medium heat.
Cover, reduce heat, and simmer 5 minutes; remove and discard onion.

Add corn to hot milk; bring to a boil. Reduce heat, and cook 5 minutes,
stirring often. Add cornstarch mixture, salt, and pepper; cook, stirring constantly, 3 minutes or until thickened and bubbly. Yield: 3 (¾-cup) servings.

Spicy-Hot Black-Eyed Peas

A splash of liquid smoke gives these peas a slow-simmered meaty flavor.

Vegetable cooking spray
½ cup chopped onion
½ cup chopped green pepper
1 (15.8-ounce) can black-eyed
   peas, undrained
1 (14½-ounce) can no-salt-added
   stewed tomatoes, undrained
1 tablespoon low-sodium soy
   sauce

1 teaspoon dry mustard
1 teaspoon liquid smoke
½ teaspoon chili powder
½ teaspoon black pepper
⅛ teaspoon ground red pepper
1 tablespoon minced fresh
   parsley

Per serving:
Calories 158 (7% from fat)
Fat 1.3g (sat 0.3g;
   mono 0.1g; poly 0.5g)
Cholesterol 0mg
Sodium 120mg
Carbohydrate 27.5g
Fiber 3.4g
Protein 10.4g

Coat a large nonstick skillet with cooking spray; place over medium heat until hot. Add onion and green pepper; cook, stirring constantly, until crisp-tender. Add peas and next 7 ingredients; bring to a boil. Reduce heat, and simmer, uncovered, 20 minutes. Sprinkle with parsley. Yield: 4 (¾-cup) servings.

Stir-Fried Snow Peas and Peppers

Fresh snow peas, red pepper strips, and water chestnuts add color and crunch to this Asian accompaniment.

Vegetable cooking spray
1 teaspoon vegetable oil
½ pound fresh snow pea pods
1½ cups julienne-sliced sweet red
   pepper
1 (8-ounce) can sliced water
   chestnuts, drained
¼ cup water

1 tablespoon low-sodium soy
   sauce
1 teaspoon sugar
½ teaspoon cornstarch
¼ teaspoon chicken-flavored
   bouillon granules
Dash of pepper
1 teaspoon sesame seeds, toasted

Per serving:
Calories 95 (19% from fat)
Fat 2.0g (sat 0.3g;
   mono 0.5g; poly 0.9g)
Cholesterol 0mg
Sodium 177mg
Carbohydrate 16.8g
Fiber 2.5g
Protein 2.8g

Coat a wok or large nonstick skillet with cooking spray; add oil. Heat at medium-high (375°) for 2 minutes. Add peas, pepper strips, and water chestnuts; stir-fry 3 to 5 minutes or until crisp-tender.

Combine water and next 5 ingredients; pour over vegetable mixture. Cook, stirring constantly, 1 minute or until thickened. Transfer to a bowl; sprinkle with sesame seeds. Serve immediately. Yield: 4 (¾-cup) servings.

Easy Spiced Baked Peaches

1 (15-ounce) can peach halves in extra light syrup, undrained
¼ cup sugar
3 tablespoons reduced-calorie margarine

2 tablespoons lemon juice
12 whole cloves
6 (3-inch) sticks cinnamon, broken into pieces
Ground nutmeg (optional)

Drain peaches, reserving syrup. Set peaches aside. Add enough water to syrup to make ⅔ cup. Combine syrup mixture, sugar, margarine, and lemon juice in a small saucepan. Cook over medium heat just until margarine melts, stirring often.

Place cloves and broken cinnamon sticks on a square of cheesecloth; tie with string. Add spice bag to syrup mixture; bring to a boil. Reduce heat, and simmer, uncovered, 15 minutes. Remove and discard spice bag.

Place peach halves, cut sides up, in an ungreased 1-quart baking dish. Spoon syrup mixture over peaches. Bake, uncovered, at 350° for 20 minutes. Sprinkle with nutmeg, if desired. Yield: 4 servings.

Tropical Fresh Fruit Compote

When you crave something besides an ordinary
green salad to round out the meal, try this fruity side.
It's even perfect for a light, summery dessert.

2½ cups cubed fresh pineapple
1 large seedless orange, peeled and sectioned
1 medium apple, cut into ¾-inch cubes
1 small banana, sliced

1 ripe papaya, peeled and cut into ¾-inch cubes
¼ cup Grand Marnier or other orange-flavored liqueur
¼ cup unsweetened orange juice

Combine first 5 ingredients in a large bowl, tossing gently.

Combine liqueur and orange juice; pour over fruit, and toss gently. Cover and chill at least 1 hour. Yield: 10 (¾-cup) servings.

Dried Apple Side Dish

Dried Apple Side Dish

*Your taste buds might fool you on this recipe. This
buttery-tasting fruit side is very low in fat and short on
cooking time. It's ready, start to finish, in 30 minutes.*

1 (6-ounce) package sliced dried
    apples
2½ cups water
¾ cup raisins

½ cup firmly packed brown sugar
1 tablespoon reduced-calorie
    margarine
¼ teaspoon butter flavoring

Per serving:
Calories 192 (6% from fat)
Fat 1.3g (sat 0.2g;
   mono 0.0g; poly 0.0g)
Cholesterol 0mg
Sodium 260mg
Carbohydrate 49.2g
Fiber 4.7g
Protein 0.6g

Combine apple slices and water in a medium saucepan; bring to a boil. Reduce
heat, and simmer, uncovered, 25 minutes.

    Stir in raisins and remaining ingredients; cook, uncovered, 5 minutes, stir-
ring occasionally. Yield: 6 (½-cup) servings.

Brown Rice Pilaf

Brown rice and toasted almonds team up for
a nutty flavor combo in this side dish.

2 cups canned no-salt-added
 chicken broth, undiluted
1 cup brown rice, uncooked
½ cup shredded carrot
½ cup finely chopped celery
¼ cup finely sliced green onions

½ teaspoon salt
¼ teaspoon ground red pepper
1 clove garlic, minced
3 tablespoons slivered almonds,
 toasted

Bring broth to a boil in a heavy saucepan; stir in rice and remaining ingredients, except almonds. Cover, reduce heat, and simmer 50 to 55 minutes or until rice is tender and liquid is absorbed. Stir in almonds. Serve immediately. Yield: 8 (½-cup) servings.

Garlic and Lemon Linguine

Recipes don't get much easier or tastier than this.
If you have the time, grate fresh Parmesan cheese
and squeeze lemon juice for maximum flavor.

1½ tablespoons reduced-calorie
 margarine
¼ cup grated Parmesan cheese
2 tablespoons lemon juice

½ teaspoon pepper
2 cloves garlic, crushed
2½ cups hot cooked linguine
 (cooked without salt or fat)

Melt margarine in a small saucepan over medium heat; stir in Parmesan cheese and next 3 ingredients. Pour over pasta; toss gently. Serve immediately. Yield: 5 (½-cup) servings.

Linguine with Red Pepper Sauce

Linguine with Red Pepper Sauce

The natural sweetness of red peppers, balsamic vinegar, and fresh basil adds flair to the thick, rich sauce that tops this pasta. We liked this recipe so much that as soon as we tasted it, we jotted it down to slip into our own files.

Vegetable cooking spray
2 teaspoons olive oil
3 cups chopped sweet red pepper
2 small cloves garlic, crushed
⅓ cup chopped fresh basil

¼ cup balsamic vinegar
¼ teaspoon salt
⅛ teaspoon pepper
6 cups hot cooked linguine
Garnish: fresh basil sprigs

Per serving:
Calories 240 (10% from fat)
Fat 2.7g (sat 0.4g;
  mono 1.2g; poly 0.6g)
Cholesterol 0mg
Sodium 104mg
Carbohydrate 45.8g
Fiber 2.2g
Protein 7.9g

Coat a nonstick skillet with cooking spray; add oil. Place over medium heat until hot. Add sweet red pepper and garlic; cook, uncovered, 30 minutes, stirring occasionally. Set aside, and cool slightly.

Place pepper mixture in container of an electric blender or food processor; add chopped basil and next 3 ingredients. Cover and process until smooth, stopping once to scrape down sides. For each serving, top 1 cup pasta with ¼ cup pepper sauce. Garnish, if desired. Serve immediately. Yield: 6 servings.

Pasta Provençal

One side dish is all you'll need with this clever combination of twirled pasta and fresh vegetables.

Per serving:
Calories 109 (31% from fat)
Fat 3.8g (sat 1.0g;
  mono 2.0g; poly 0.4g)
Cholesterol 3mg
Sodium 338mg
Carbohydrate 15.4g
Fiber 1.5g
Protein 4.5g

1 tablespoon olive oil
3 cups sliced zucchini
1 cup sliced fresh mushrooms
½ cup chopped green pepper
¼ cup chopped onion
1 clove garlic, minced
1 (14½-ounce) can stewed
  tomatoes, undrained and
  chopped
¾ teaspoon chopped fresh basil
  or ¼ teaspoon dried basil

½ teaspoon chopped fresh
  oregano or ⅛ teaspoon dried
  oregano
¼ teaspoon salt
¼ teaspoon pepper
2 cups hot cooked rotini noodles
  (cooked without salt or fat)
¼ cup grated Parmesan cheese

Heat olive oil in a Dutch oven over medium heat. Add zucchini and next 4 ingredients to Dutch oven; cook, stirring constantly, 5 minutes. Add tomato and next 4 ingredients; bring to a boil, and remove from heat. Add pasta and cheese; toss gently. Serve immediately. Yield: 6 (1-cup) servings.

Vermicelli with Tomato-Basil Sauce

A trip to the garden or farmers market for ripe red tomatoes and fresh basil will yield a pasta sauce that boasts a bounty of summertime flavors.

Per serving:
Calories 163 (10% from fat)
Fat 1.9g (sat 0.6g;
  mono 0.3g; poly 0.2g)
Cholesterol 2mg
Sodium 147mg
Carbohydrate 29.9g
Fiber 2.9g
Protein 6.3g

8 ounces vermicelli, uncooked
Vegetable cooking spray
2 cloves garlic, minced
1 medium onion, thinly sliced
5 cups peeled, chopped
  tomato (about 5 medium
  tomatoes)

¼ cup minced fresh basil
¼ teaspoon salt
⅛ teaspoon pepper
1 (8-ounce) can no-salt-added
  tomato sauce
¼ cup freshly grated Parmesan
  cheese

Cook pasta according to package directions, omitting salt and fat. Drain.
  Coat a Dutch oven with cooking spray; place over medium heat until hot.
Add garlic and onion; cook, stirring constantly, 5 minutes or until onion is

tender. Stir in tomato and next 4 ingredients; bring to a boil. Reduce heat, and simmer, uncovered, 15 minutes, stirring occasionally.

Add cooked pasta to tomato mixture; cook, uncovered, until mixture is thoroughly heated, stirring occasionally. Sprinkle with cheese. Serve immediately. Yield: 8 (1-cup) servings.

Macaroni and Cheese

Mention "macaroni and cheese," and visions of creamy, cheesy, down-home goodness pop into most minds. Our lightened version of this revered comfort food will meet your highest expectations.

1 (8-ounce) package elbow
   macaroni
2 tablespoons reduced-calorie
   margarine
2 tablespoons all-purpose flour
2 cups skim milk
1½ cups (6 ounces) shredded
   reduced-fat sharp Cheddar
   cheese

½ teaspoon salt
3 tablespoons egg substitute
Vegetable cooking spray
¼ teaspoon paprika

Per serving:
Calories 111 (37% from fat)
Fat 4.6g (sat 2.0g;
   mono 0.9g; poly 0.2g)
Cholesterol 11mg
Sodium 268mg
Carbohydrate 9.8g
Fiber 0.4g
Protein 7.6g

Cook pasta according to package directions, omitting salt and fat. Drain.

Melt margarine in a heavy saucepan over low heat; add flour, stirring until smooth. Cook, stirring constantly, 1 minute. Gradually add milk; cook over medium heat, stirring constantly, until thickened and bubbly. Add cheese and salt, stirring until cheese melts. Gradually stir about one-fourth of hot mixture into egg substitute. Add to remaining hot mixture, stirring constantly.

Combine cheese sauce and pasta; pour into a 2-quart baking dish coated with cooking spray. Sprinkle with paprika. Bake at 350° for 25 to 30 minutes or until thoroughly heated. Yield: 11 (½-cup) servings.

BREADS

You'd know that aroma anywhere—that of home-made bread baking in the oven. Whether you prefer soft and tender quick breads or warm and crusty yeast breads, we've got your number. How about melt-in-your-mouth Light Biscuits or Fruity Banana Bread? They're quick to fix and guaranteed family pleasers. Speaking of quick, try Parsley-Garlic Rolls, which make use of convenient frozen bread dough. And our yeast breads will bring rave reviews; nearly all of them received our highest rating.

Old-Fashioned Cinnamon Rolls (page 211)

Granola Muffins

With ingredients like granola cereal, raisins, brown sugar, and cinnamon, these substantial muffins are sure to satisfy. Keep a few on hand in the freezer to enjoy for a spur-of-the-moment snack.

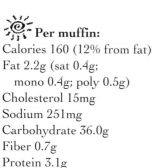
Per muffin:
Calories 160 (12% from fat)
Fat 2.2g (sat 0.4g;
    mono 0.4g; poly 0.5g)
Cholesterol 15mg
Sodium 251mg
Carbohydrate 36.0g
Fiber 0.7g
Protein 3.1g

1½ cups reduced-fat biscuit and
    baking mix
1 cup low-fat granola cereal
    without raisins
½ cup raisins
½ cup firmly packed brown
    sugar

1 teaspoon ground cinnamon
1 egg, lightly beaten
¾ cup skim milk
1 tablespoon vegetable oil
Vegetable cooking spray

Combine first 5 ingredients in a large bowl; make a well in center of mixture. Combine egg, milk, and oil; add to flour mixture, stirring just until dry ingredients are moistened. (Batter will be thin.)

Spoon batter into muffin pans coated with cooking spray, filling two-thirds full. Bake at 375° for 20 minutes or until golden. Remove muffins from pans immediately. Yield: 14 muffins.

Pumpkin-Pecan Bread

Make an extra batch of this aromatic nut bread to share during the holidays.

Per slice:
Calories 112 (30% from fat)
Fat 3.7g (sat 0.6g;
    mono 1.5g; poly 1.4g)
Cholesterol 0mg
Sodium 75mg
Carbohydrate 17.6g
Fiber 1.1g
Protein 2.4g

1¾ cups all-purpose flour
1 teaspoon baking powder
½ teaspoon baking soda
¼ teaspoon salt
½ cup sugar
¾ teaspoon ground cinnamon

½ teaspoon ground nutmeg
1 cup canned pumpkin
½ cup egg substitute
2½ tablespoons vegetable oil
¼ cup chopped pecans
Vegetable cooking spray

Combine first 7 ingredients in a large bowl; make a well in center of mixture. Combine pumpkin, egg substitute, and oil; add to flour mixture, stirring just until dry ingredients are moistened. Fold in pecans.

Spoon batter into an 8½- x 4½- x 3-inch loafpan coated with cooking spray. Bake at 350° for 45 minutes or until a wooden pick inserted in center of loaf comes out clean. Cool in pan on a wire rack 10 minutes; remove from pan, and cool completely on wire rack. Yield: 16 (½-inch) slices.

Fruity Banana Bread

Fruity Banana Bread

We took a yummy banana bread recipe, stirred in some chopped dried fruit, and came up with this quick bread that's one of our favorites.

⅓ cup margarine, softened
¾ cup sugar
½ cup egg substitute
1¾ cups all-purpose flour
2¾ teaspoons baking powder

1 cup mashed ripe banana (about 2 medium)
¾ cup coarsely chopped mixed dried fruit
Vegetable cooking spray

Per slice:
Calories 150 (24% from fat)
Fat 4.0g (sat 0.8g;
  mono 1.7g; poly 1.3g)
Cholesterol 0mg
Sodium 64mg
Carbohydrate 27.3g
Fiber 1.5g
Protein 2.2g

Beat margarine at medium speed of an electric mixer until creamy; gradually add sugar, beating well. Add egg substitute; beat just until blended.

Combine flour and baking powder; add to margarine mixture, beating at low speed just until blended. Stir in banana and dried fruit.

Spoon batter into an 8½- x 4½- x 3-inch loafpan coated with cooking spray. Bake at 350° for 1 hour or until a wooden pick inserted in center of loaf comes out clean. Cool in pan on a wire rack 10 minutes; remove from pan, and cool completely on wire rack. Yield: 16 (½-inch) slices.

Cornmeal Yeast Muffins

These dinner muffins tease you with subtle cornmeal crunch.

¾ cup skim milk
3 tablespoons sugar
2 tablespoons reduced-calorie
    margarine
2 tablespoons vegetable oil
1 package active dry yeast
¼ cup warm water (105° to 115°)

3 cups all-purpose flour, divided
¾ cup plain yellow cornmeal
½ teaspoon salt
¼ cup egg substitute
¼ cup all-purpose flour
Butter-flavored vegetable cooking
    spray

Combine first 4 ingredients in a saucepan; heat until margarine melts. Cool to 105° to 115°. Combine yeast and warm water; let stand 5 minutes.

Combine 1 cup flour, cornmeal, and salt in a mixing bowl; add milk mixture, yeast mixture, and egg substitute. Beat at medium speed of an electric mixer until smooth. Stir in enough of 2 cups flour to make a soft dough.

Sprinkle ¼ cup flour evenly over work surface. Turn dough out onto floured surface, and knead until smooth and elastic (about 8 minutes). Place in a bowl coated with cooking spray; turn to coat top. Cover; let rise in a warm place (85°), free from drafts, 1 hour or until doubled in bulk.

Punch dough down; divide into fourths. Divide and shape each fourth into 9 balls. Place 2 balls in each muffin cup coated with cooking spray. Cover and let rise in a warm place, free from drafts, 15 minutes or until doubled in bulk. Bake at 375° for 12 to 15 minutes or until golden. Spray muffin tops lightly with cooking spray; remove muffins from pans immediately. Yield: 1½ dozen.

Rosemary Focaccia

1 package active dry yeast
1¼ cups warm water (105° to
    115°), divided
3¾ cups all-purpose flour, divided
1 teaspoon salt, divided
3 tablespoons margarine, melted

½ cup chopped fresh rosemary,
    divided
2 tablespoons all-purpose flour
Olive oil-flavored vegetable
    cooking spray
4 cloves garlic, minced

Combine yeast and ¼ cup warm water; let stand 5 minutes. Combine yeast mixture, remaining 1 cup warm water, 2 cups flour, and ½ teaspoon salt in a

Rosemary Focaccia

large mixing bowl; beat at medium speed of an electric mixer until mixture is well blended. Cover and let rise in a warm place (85°), free from drafts, 1 hour or until doubled in bulk.

Punch dough down; stir in 1¾ cups flour, melted margarine, and ¼ cup rosemary.

Sprinkle 2 tablespoons flour evenly over work surface. Turn dough out onto floured surface, and knead until smooth and elastic (about 10 minutes). Divide dough in half. For each focaccia, roll or press 1 portion of dough into an 11-inch circle on a baking sheet coated with cooking spray. Poke holes in dough at 1-inch intervals with handle of a wooden spoon.

Coat top of each round with cooking spray; sprinkle evenly with remaining ¼ cup rosemary, remaining ½ teaspoon salt, and garlic. Bake at 400° for 20 minutes. Cut each circle into 12 squares or wedges. Yield: 24 servings.

Honey-Oat Bread

We're pretty stingy when it comes to giving recipes our highest rating. But when a best-of-show bread like this one comes along, we're quick to give it the accolades it deserves.

Per slice:
Calories 134 (25% from fat)
Fat 3.7g (sat 0.6g;
   mono 1.0g; poly 1.7g)
Cholesterol 0mg
Sodium 105mg
Carbohydrate 21.9g
Fiber 1.6g
Protein 3.9g

1¾ cups water
½ cup vegetable oil
½ cup honey
3⅔ cups bread flour, divided
1 cup regular oats, uncooked
½ cup unprocessed oat bran
1½ teaspoons salt

2 packages active dry yeast
½ cup egg substitute
2½ cups whole wheat flour
½ cup bread flour
Vegetable cooking spray
1 egg white, lightly beaten
1 tablespoon water

Combine first 3 ingredients in a medium saucepan; heat to 120° to 130°.

Combine 1⅔ cups bread flour, oats, and next 3 ingredients in a large mixing bowl; gradually add honey mixture, beating at low speed of an electric mixer until blended. Beat 2 additional minutes at medium speed. Add egg substitute; beat well. Gradually add whole wheat flour, beating 2 minutes at medium speed. Gradually stir in enough of 2 cups bread flour to make a soft dough.

Sprinkle ½ cup bread flour evenly over work surface. Turn dough out onto floured surface, and knead until smooth and elastic (about 10 minutes). Place dough in a large bowl coated with cooking spray, turning to coat top. Cover and let rise in a warm place (85°), free from drafts, 1 hour or until doubled in bulk.

Punch dough down; turn out onto work surface, and knead lightly 4 or 5 times. Divide dough in half. Roll 1 portion of dough into a 14- x 7-inch rectangle. Roll up dough, starting at short side, pressing firmly to eliminate air pockets; pinch ends to seal. Place dough, seam side down, in a 9- x 5- x 3-inch loafpan coated with cooking spray. Repeat procedure with remaining portion of dough.

Cover and let rise in a warm place, free from drafts, 30 minutes or until doubled in bulk.

Combine egg white and 1 tablespoon water; gently brush egg white mixture evenly over loaves. Bake at 375° for 35 minutes or until loaves sound hollow when tapped. (Cover loaves with aluminum foil the last 15 to 20 minutes of baking to prevent excessive browning, if necessary.) Remove from pans; cool on wire racks. Yield: 36 (½-inch) slices.

Onion-Herb Bread

3 packages active dry yeast

4 cups warm water (105° to 115°), divided

4 cups whole wheat flour

1 cup diced onion

½ cup instant nonfat dry milk powder

⅓ cup sugar

¼ cup vegetable oil

1½ tablespoons chopped fresh dillweed

1 tablespoon chopped fresh rosemary

2 teaspoons salt

6¼ to 6½ cups all-purpose flour

2 tablespoons all-purpose flour

Butter-flavored vegetable cooking spray

Per slice:
Calories 104 (12% from fat)
Fat 1.4g (sat 0.2g; mono 0.3g; poly 0.6g)
Cholesterol 0mg
Sodium 94mg
Carbohydrate 19.9g
Fiber 1.7g
Protein 3.3g

Combine yeast and 1 cup warm water in a 2-cup liquid measuring cup; let stand 5 minutes.

Combine yeast mixture, remaining 3 cups warm water, whole wheat flour, and next 7 ingredients in a large mixing bowl. Beat at medium speed of an electric mixer until well blended. Gradually stir in enough of 6¼ to 6½ cups all-purpose flour to make a soft dough.

Sprinkle 2 tablespoons all-purpose flour evenly over work surface. Turn dough out onto floured surface, and knead until smooth and elastic (about 10 minutes). Place in a bowl coated with cooking spray, turning to coat top. Cover and let rise in a warm place (85°), free from drafts, 35 minutes or until doubled in bulk.

Punch dough down, and divide into thirds. Roll 1 portion of dough into a 14- x 7-inch rectangle. Roll up dough, starting at short side, pressing firmly to eliminate air pockets; pinch ends to seal. Place dough, seam side down, in a 9- x 5- x 3-inch loafpan coated with cooking spray. Repeat procedure with remaining 2 portions of dough.

Cover and let rise in a warm place, free from drafts, 30 minutes or until doubled in bulk. Bake at 350° for 40 to 45 minutes or until loaves sound hollow when tapped. Coat tops of loaves with cooking spray. Remove loaves from pans immediately; cool on wire racks. Yield: 54 (½-inch) slices.

Cornmeal Yeast Bread

Cornmeal Yeast Bread

*A thick slice of this slightly sweet, slightly crunchy bread
will accompany a steaming bowl of chowder perfectly.*

Per slice:
Calories 77 (20% from fat)
Fat 1.7g (sat 0.3g;
    mono 0.1g; poly 0.1g)
Cholesterol 7mg
Sodium 102mg
Carbohydrate 13.5g
Fiber 0.7g
Protein 2.2g

¾ cup evaporated skimmed milk
⅓ cup sugar
⅓ cup reduced-calorie margarine
1 teaspoon salt
2 packages active dry yeast
½ cup warm water (105° to 115°)

3 to 3½ cups all-purpose flour,
    divided
¾ cup yellow cornmeal
1 egg
1 tablespoon all-purpose flour
Vegetable cooking spray

Combine first 4 ingredients in a saucepan; heat until margarine melts. Cool to
105° to 115°. Combine yeast and warm water; let stand 5 minutes.

Combine milk mixture, yeast mixture, 1 cup flour, cornmeal, and egg in a
large mixing bowl; beat mixture at medium speed of an electric mixer until well
blended. Gradually stir in enough of 2 to 2½ cups flour to make a soft dough.

Sprinkle 1 tablespoon flour evenly over work surface. Turn dough out
onto floured surface, and knead until smooth and elastic (about 10 minutes).
Place in a bowl coated with cooking spray; turn to coat top. Cover; let rise in
a warm place (85°), free from drafts, 1 hour or until doubled in bulk.

Punch dough down; divide in half. Roll 1 portion into a 14- x 7-inch rectangle. Roll up, starting at short side, pressing firmly to eliminate air pockets; pinch ends to seal. Place, seam side down, in an 8½- x 4½- x 3-inch loafpan coated with cooking spray. Repeat procedure with remaining dough.

Cover and let rise in a warm place, free from drafts, 45 minutes or until doubled in bulk. Bake at 350° for 30 to 35 minutes or until loaves sound hollow when tapped. Remove from pans immediately, and cool on wire racks. Yield: 32 (½-inch) slices.

French Bread

The contrast of this bread's soft inside to its crusty outside is what makes folks enjoy it so much.

1 cup water	1 package active dry yeast
¼ cup skim milk	3¼ to 3½ cups all-purpose flour,
1 tablespoon plus 1 teaspoon	divided
sugar	2 tablespoons all-purpose flour
1 tablespoon reduced-calorie	Vegetable cooking spray
margarine	1 egg white, lightly beaten
1 teaspoon salt	1 tablespoon water

Per slice:
Calories 24 (8% from fat)
Fat 0.2g (sat 0.0g;
   mono 0.0g; poly 0.0g)
Cholesterol 0mg
Sodium 37mg
Carbohydrate 4.7g
Fiber 0.2g
Protein 0.7g

Combine first 5 ingredients in a saucepan; heat until margarine melts. Cool to 105° to 115°. Add yeast to warm milk mixture; let stand 5 minutes.

Combine 1¼ cups flour and yeast mixture in a large mixing bowl; beat at medium speed of an electric mixer until blended. Stir in enough of 2 to 2¼ cups flour to make a soft dough; let stand 10 minutes. Stir dough gently for a few seconds; cover and let stand 40 minutes, stirring every 10 minutes.

Sprinkle 2 tablespoons flour evenly over work surface. Turn dough out onto floured surface, and divide in half. Flatten 1 portion of dough into an oval on floured surface. Fold dough over lengthwise, and flatten with open hand. Fold again, and roll between palms of hands into a 17-inch rope. Pinch ends of rope to seal. Repeat procedure with remaining portion of dough.

Place dough in two French bread pans coated with cooking spray. Using a sharp knife, cut ½-inch-deep slits across tops of loaves. Cover and let rise in a warm place (85°), free from drafts, 20 minutes or until loaves are doubled in bulk. Combine egg white and 1 tablespoon water; brush mixture evenly over loaves. Bake at 400° for 15 minutes or until loaves sound hollow when tapped. Yield: 68 (½-inch) slices.

DESSERTS

*I*f you're one of those folks who likes a little something sweet but with little fat and even fewer calories, then you're in for a treat. You *can* have your cake and eat it, too. Light Hummingbird Cake, our new version of the most requested recipe ever from *Southern Living*, proves it. If your heart desires dessert like Mom used to make, then dive into Old-Fashioned Banana Pudding. And don't miss out on Chocolate-Almond Cheesecake. One bite will tell you why we rated it our biggest temptation.

Chocolate-Almond Cheesecake (page 227)

Bird's Nest Cookies

Sweet, crisp shells cradle colorful candy "eggs" in this kids'
favorite. Try pastel candies at Easter for a springtime look.

Per cookie:
Calories 63 (26% from fat)
Fat 1.8g (sat 0.7g;
    mono 0.0g; poly 0.0g)
Cholesterol 1mg
Sodium 10mg
Carbohydrate 47.0g
Fiber 0.6g
Protein 1.2g

2 egg whites
¾ teaspoon vanilla extract
½ teaspoon ground cinnamon
⅛ teaspoon cream of tartar
Dash of salt
⅔ cup sugar

6 large shredded whole wheat
    cereal biscuits, crushed
Vegetable cooking spray
1¼ cups candy-coated
    chocolate-covered peanuts
    (about 8½ ounces)

Combine first 5 ingredients in a small mixing bowl; beat at high speed of an electric mixer until foamy. Gradually add sugar, 1 tablespoon at a time, beating until stiff peaks form and sugar dissolves (2 to 4 minutes). Stir in cereal.

Drop mixture by level tablespoonfuls onto cookie sheets coated with cooking spray. Make an indentation in center of each cookie with the back of a teaspoon; place 3 peanut candies in each indentation.

Bake at 275° for 30 minutes. Transfer cookies immediately to wire racks; cool. Store in an airtight container. Yield: 3 dozen.

Apricot-Raisin Bars

Per bar:
Calories 93 (26% from fat)
Fat 2.7g (sat 0.5g;
    mono 0.8g; poly 1.2g)
Cholesterol 9mg
Sodium 33mg
Carbohydrate 16.5g
Fiber 0.9g
Protein 1.4g

1 egg, lightly beaten
¼ cup vegetable oil
¼ cup molasses
1 teaspoon vanilla extract
1½ cups all-purpose flour
2 teaspoons baking powder

¼ teaspoon salt
1 teaspoon apple pie spice
1¼ cups peeled, grated apple
¾ cup chopped dried apricot
¾ cup raisins
Vegetable cooking spray

Combine first 4 ingredients in a medium bowl. Combine flour and next 3 ingredients; add to molasses mixture, stirring well. (Batter will be very thick.) Stir in grated apple, chopped apricot, and raisins.

Spread mixture in a 9-inch square pan coated with cooking spray. Bake at 350° for 20 minutes or until a wooden pick inserted in center comes out clean. Cool in pan on a wire rack; cut into bars. Yield: 2 dozen.

No-Bake Chocolate-Kahlúa Balls

For a no-fuss dessert, roll spoonfuls of this rich, chocolaty dough into bite-size balls. No food processor? No problem. Simply crush the little cookies, and knead the mixture together with your hands.

1 (10-ounce) package teddy bear-shaped chocolate graham cracker cookies
⅔ cup finely chopped pitted whole dates
¼ cup instant nonfat dry milk powder

3 tablespoons Kahlúa or other coffee-flavored liqueur
2 tablespoons skim milk
⅓ cup finely chopped pecans

Per ball:
Calories 42 (32% from fat)
Fat 1.5g (sat 0.2g;
    mono 0.6g; poly 0.1g)
Cholesterol 0mg
Sodium 32mg
Carbohydrate 6.4g
Fiber 0.4g
Protein 0.7g

Position knife blade in food processor bowl; add cookies. Process until mixture is a fine powder. With processor running, add dates and next 3 ingredients to processor bowl through food chute; blend just until smooth. Shape mixture into ¾-inch balls; roll in pecans. Cover and chill. Yield: 4 dozen.

Chocolate Angel Food Cake

This heavenly cake is as guilt free as it gets when it comes to indulging in desserts.

1¼ cups sugar, divided
1 cup sifted cake flour
¼ cup cocoa
12 egg whites

1½ teaspoons cream of tartar
¼ teaspoon salt
1 teaspoon vanilla extract
½ teaspoon almond extract

Per serving:
Calories 140 (2% from fat)
Fat 0.3g (sat 0.2g;
    mono 0.0g; poly 0.0g)
Cholesterol 0mg
Sodium 103mg
Carbohydrate 29.4g
Fiber 0.0g
Protein 4.6g

Sift ¼ cup sugar, flour, and cocoa together into a small bowl; set aside.

Beat egg whites in a mixing bowl at high speed of an electric mixer until foamy. Add cream of tartar and salt, and beat until soft peaks form. Add 1 cup sugar, 2 tablespoons at a time, beating until stiff peaks form and sugar dissolves.

Sift flour mixture over egg white mixture, ¼ cup at a time, folding in after each addition. Fold in flavorings. Spoon batter evenly into an ungreased 10-inch tube pan. Break air pockets by cutting through batter with a knife. Bake at 375° for 30 minutes or until cake springs back when lightly touched.

Remove cake from oven; invert pan, and cool. Loosen cake from pan, using a narrow metal spatula; remove cake from pan. Yield: 12 servings.

Old-Fashioned Strawberry Shortcake

Old-Fashioned Strawberry Shortcake

Ruby-red strawberries float on a billowy cloud of whipped topping and oh-so-sweet cake layers in this all-time favorite.

Per serving:
Calories 260 (27% from fat)
Fat 7.7g (sat 2.2g;
  mono 2.5g; poly 1.9g)
Cholesterol 25mg
Sodium 158mg
Carbohydrate 43.3g
Fiber 2.3g
Protein 5.1g

4 cups sliced fresh strawberries
¼ cup sugar
Vegetable cooking spray
2 teaspoons all-purpose flour
1¾ cups all-purpose flour
2½ teaspoons baking powder
¼ teaspoon salt
¼ cup margarine, softened
⅓ cup sugar

1 egg yolk
¾ cup skim milk
½ teaspoon vanilla extract
2 egg whites
2 tablespoons sugar
1½ cups reduced-calorie frozen
  whipped topping, thawed
Garnish: fresh strawberry leaves
  or mint sprigs

Combine strawberries and ¼ cup sugar; cover and chill 2 hours, stirring occasionally.

Coat a 9-inch round cakepan with cooking spray; dust pan with 2 teaspoons flour, and set aside. Combine 1¾ cups flour, baking powder, and salt; set aside.

Beat margarine at medium speed of an electric mixer until creamy; gradually add ⅓ cup sugar, beating well. Add egg yolk, beating just until blended. Add flour mixture to margarine mixture alternately with milk, beginning and ending with flour mixture. Mix at low speed after each addition until blended. Stir in vanilla.

Beat egg whites at high speed of mixer until foamy. Gradually add 2 tablespoons sugar, beating until stiff peaks form and sugar dissolves (2 to 4 minutes). Fold about one-fourth of egg white mixture into flour mixture. Gently fold in remaining egg white mixture.

Spoon batter into prepared pan. Bake at 350° for 30 minutes or until a wooden pick inserted in center comes out clean. Cool in pan on a wire rack 10 minutes; remove from pan, and cool completely on wire rack.

Slice cake layer in half horizontally; place bottom half, cut side up, on a serving plate. Drain strawberry mixture, reserving juice; drizzle half of juice over bottom cake layer. Spread ⅔ cup whipped topping over cake layer, and top with half of drained strawberries.

Position remaining cake layer, cut side down, over strawberries; drizzle with remaining strawberry juice. Spread cake layer with ¾ cup whipped topping; top with remaining strawberries. Dollop remaining whipped topping on top, and garnish, if desired. Yield: 9 servings.

Lemon-Poppy Seed Cake

1 cup egg substitute
½ cup sugar
⅓ cup vegetable oil
¼ cup water
3 tablespoons lemon juice
1 (18.25-ounce) package reduced-fat yellow cake mix
1 (8-ounce) carton vanilla nonfat yogurt
2 tablespoons poppy seeds
Vegetable cooking spray
½ cup sifted powdered sugar
2 tablespoons lemon juice

Per serving:
Calories 171 (32% from fat)
Fat 6.0g (sat 1.3g;
   mono 0.9g; poly 1.7g)
Cholesterol 0mg
Sodium 22mg
Carbohydrate 8.8g
Fiber 0.0g
Protein 1.6g

Combine first 7 ingredients in a large mixing bowl; beat at medium speed of an electric mixer 6 minutes. Stir in poppy seeds.

Pour batter into a 10-cup Bundt pan coated with cooking spray. Bake at 350° for 50 minutes or until a wooden pick inserted in center comes out clean. Cool in pan on a wire rack 10 minutes.

Combine powdered sugar and 2 tablespoons lemon juice. Place a sheet of wax paper under wire rack; remove cake from pan, and place on wire rack. Brush cake with glaze; cool completely. Yield: 24 servings.

Spice Cake with Coffee Frosting

*Nonfat mayonnaise makes this cake as rich and moist as
traditional butter-based cakes, but without the fat and calories.
And the frosting is delightfully sweet and silky.*

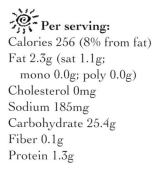 **Per serving:**
Calories 256 (8% from fat)
Fat 2.3g (sat 1.1g;
   mono 0.0g; poly 0.0g)
Cholesterol 0mg
Sodium 185mg
Carbohydrate 25.4g
Fiber 0.1g
Protein 1.3g

1¾ cups water
⅔ cup nonfat mayonnaise
1 teaspoon ground cinnamon
½ teaspoon ground allspice
½ teaspoon ground ginger
⅛ teaspoon ground nutmeg

3 egg whites
1 (18.25-ounce) package
   reduced-fat yellow cake mix
Vegetable cooking spray
Coffee Frosting

Combine first 8 ingredients in a large mixing bowl; beat at low speed of an
electric mixer until blended. Beat at high speed 2 minutes.

   Pour batter into two 9-inch round cakepans coated with cooking spray.
Bake at 350° for 30 to 35 minutes or until a wooden pick inserted in center
comes out clean. Cool layers in pans on wire racks 10 minutes; remove from
pans, and cool completely on wire racks. Spread Coffee Frosting between
layers and on top and sides of cake. Yield: 14 servings.

Coffee Frosting

2 teaspoons instant coffee
   granules
¼ cup plus 1 tablespoon warm
   water
1½ cups sugar

1 tablespoon light corn syrup
Dash of salt
2 egg whites
1 teaspoon vanilla extract

Combine coffee granules and warm water; stir until granules dissolve. Combine coffee, sugar, and next 3 ingredients in top of a large double boiler; beat
at low speed of an electric mixer 30 seconds or just until blended.

   Place double boiler over boiling water; beat mixture at high speed 11 to 12
minutes or until stiff peaks form and temperature reaches 160°. Remove pan
from heat. Add vanilla, and beat 2 additional minutes or until frosting is
spreading consistency. Yield: 4¼ cups.

Light Hummingbird Cake

Here it is: the all-new lightened version of the most-requested recipe ever from Southern Living! *We conducted a side-by-side taste test comparing this cake with its high-fat, high-calorie counterpart, and guess what? Most of our staff preferred the lightened version. Indulge!*

Vegetable cooking spray
3 cups plus 2 teaspoons
   all-purpose flour, divided
1 teaspoon baking soda
½ teaspoon salt
1¾ cups sugar
1 teaspoon ground cinnamon
2 eggs, lightly beaten

½ cup unsweetened applesauce
3 tablespoons vegetable oil
1¾ cups mashed banana
1½ teaspoons vanilla extract
1 (8-ounce) can crushed pineapple
   in juice, undrained
Cream Cheese Frosting

Coat three 9-inch round cakepans with cooking spray; sprinkle 2 teaspoons flour evenly into pans, and shake to coat. Set pans aside.

Combine remaining 3 cups flour, soda, and next 3 ingredients in a large bowl. Combine eggs, applesauce, and oil; add to flour mixture, stirring just until dry ingredients are moistened. (Do not beat.) Stir in banana, vanilla, and pineapple.

Pour batter into prepared pans. Bake at 350° for 23 to 25 minutes or until a wooden pick inserted in center comes out clean. Cool layers in pans on wire racks 10 minutes; remove layers from pans, and cool completely on wire racks. Spread Cream Cheese Frosting between layers and on top and sides of cake. Yield: 20 servings.

Cream Cheese Frosting

1 (8-ounce) package Neufchâtel
   cheese (do not soften)
1 tablespoon light butter (do not
   soften)

4 cups plus 2 tablespoons
   powdered sugar, sifted
1 teaspoon vanilla extract
¾ cup chopped pecans, toasted

Beat cheese and butter at high speed of an electric mixer until soft and creamy. Gradually add sugar, beating at low speed just until mixture is light. Gently stir in vanilla and pecans. Yield: 2⅔ cups.

Strawberry Yogurt Layer Cake

Pretty in pink describes this frosty summertime treat.

Per serving:
Calories 327 (21% from fat)
Fat 7.5g (sat 1.3g;
    mono 0.0g; poly 0.0g)
Cholesterol 0mg
Sodium 313mg
Carbohydrate 58.8g
Fiber 0.1g
Protein 5.3g

1 (18.25-ounce) package
    reduced-fat white cake mix
Vegetable cooking spray
½ gallon strawberry nonfat
    frozen yogurt, softened

3 cups reduced-calorie frozen
    whipped topping, thawed
Garnish: fresh strawberries

Prepare and bake cake mix according to package directions, using two 9-inch round cakepans coated with cooking spray. Cool in pans on wire racks 10 minutes. Remove from pans; cool completely on wire racks.

Slice cake layers in half horizontally to make 4 layers. Place bottom layer, cut side up, on a plate; spread with one-third of yogurt. Freeze. Add second cake layer; spread with one-third of yogurt. Freeze. Add third cake layer; spread with remaining yogurt. Place top cake layer, cut side down, on yogurt. Cover and freeze several hours. Spread whipped topping on top and sides of cake; cover and freeze until firm. Garnish, if desired. Yield: 14 servings.

Frosted Carrot Cake

The hint of orange is unexpected in this cake's creamy frosting.

Per serving:
Calories 212 (24% from fat)
Fat 5.6g (sat 2.4g;
    mono 1.6g; poly 1.3g)
Cholesterol 10mg
Sodium 284mg
Carbohydrate 35.7g
Fiber 1.4g
Protein 5.3g

1 (8-ounce) can crushed pineapple
    in juice, drained
2 cups grated carrot
1 cup firmly packed brown sugar
¾ cup egg substitute
¾ cup nonfat buttermilk
⅓ cup raisins
3 tablespoons vegetable oil

2 teaspoons vanilla extract
1½ cups all-purpose flour
⅔ cup whole wheat flour
2 teaspoons baking soda
¼ teaspoon salt
2 teaspoons ground cinnamon
Vegetable cooking spray
Orange-Cream Cheese Frosting

Combine first 8 ingredients in a bowl. Combine flours and next 3 ingredients; add to carrot mixture. Beat at medium speed of an electric mixer until blended.

Pour batter into a 13- x 9- x 2-inch pan coated with cooking spray. Bake at 350° for 25 to 30 minutes or until a wooden pick inserted in center comes out clean. Cool completely in pan on a wire rack. Spread Orange-Cream Cheese Frosting over top. Cover; chill until ready to serve. Yield: 18 servings.

Orange-Cream Cheese Frosting

½ cup 1% low-fat cottage cheese
1 (8-ounce) package Neufchâtel
   cheese, softened

2 teaspoons vanilla extract
1 teaspoon grated orange rind
1 cup sifted powdered sugar

Position knife blade in food processor bowl; add cottage cheese, and process 1 minute or until very smooth. Add cream cheese, vanilla, and rind; process until smooth. Add sugar; pulse 3 to 5 times or until smooth. Yield: 1½ cups.

Chocolate-Almond Cheesecake

This velvety, amaretto-laced cheesecake is our favorite dessert in this chapter.

Vegetable cooking spray
¾ cup teddy bear-shaped
   chocolate graham cracker
   cookies, finely crushed
1 (12-ounce) container 1% low-fat
   cottage cheese
⅔ cup cocoa
⅓ cup all-purpose flour
1 (8-ounce) container light process
   cream cheese, softened
1 (8-ounce) package fat-free cream
   cheese, softened

1½ cups sugar
¼ cup amaretto or other
   almond-flavored liqueur
2 teaspoons vanilla extract
1 egg
1 egg white
1 cup reduced-calorie frozen
   whipped topping, thawed
2 tablespoons sliced natural
   almonds, lightly toasted

Per serving:
Calories 206 (21% from fat)
Fat 4.9g (sat 2.4g;
   mono 0.4g; poly 0.2g)
Cholesterol 26mg
Sodium 289mg
Carbohydrate 29.6g
Fiber 0.2g
Protein 8.8g

Coat the bottom of a 9-inch springform pan with cooking spray; sprinkle half of crushed cookies over bottom of pan.

Process cottage cheese in an electric blender 2 to 3 minutes or until very smooth, scraping sides often; set aside. Sift cocoa and flour together; set aside.

Beat cream cheeses in a large bowl at medium speed of an electric mixer 10 minutes. Gradually add sugar, beating until well blended. Add cottage cheese; beat 1 minute. Add cocoa mixture; beat 1 minute, scraping sides of bowl as needed. Add amaretto and next 3 ingredients; beat 1 minute or until blended. Pour into prepared pan. Bake, uncovered, at 300° for 55 minutes or until set. Remove from oven; sprinkle with remaining crushed cookies. Run a knife around edge of pan; cool in pan on a wire rack. Cover and chill at least 8 hours.

To serve, remove sides of pan; place cheesecake on a plate. Pipe or dollop whipped topping around edge, and decorate with almonds. Yield: 16 servings.

Old-Fashioned Banana Pudding

*Simply mention the words "homemade banana pudding," and you'll see
eyes sparkle and faces light up. This recipe lives up to those expectations.*

Per serving:
Calories 212 (12% from fat)
Fat 2.8g (sat 0.6g;
  mono 0.0g; poly 0.0g)
Cholesterol 2mg
Sodium 135mg
Carbohydrate 39.8g
Fiber 1.2g
Protein 7.0g

½ cup sugar
3 tablespoons cornstarch
⅓ cup water
⅓ cup egg substitute
1 (12-ounce) can evaporated
  skimmed milk
½ cup nonfat sour cream

1 teaspoon vanilla extract
29 vanilla wafers
3 medium bananas, sliced
2 egg whites
¼ teaspoon cream of tartar
1 tablespoon sugar

Combine ½ cup sugar and cornstarch in a medium-size heavy saucepan;
gradually stir in water, egg substitute, and milk. Bring to a boil over medium
heat, stirring constantly. Boil, stirring constantly, 1 minute. Remove from
heat; fold in sour cream and vanilla.

Old-Fashioned Banana Pudding

Place a layer of vanilla wafers in bottom of a 1½-quart casserole, and spoon one-third of pudding over wafers. Top pudding with half of banana slices. Repeat layers. Spread remaining pudding over top. Arrange remaining vanilla wafers in pudding around edge of dish. Set aside.

Beat egg whites and cream of tartar at high speed of an electric mixer until foamy. Add 1 tablespoon sugar; beat until stiff peaks form and sugar dissolves (about 2 minutes). Spread meringue over pudding, sealing to wafers. Bake at 325° for 25 minutes. Let pudding stand 10 minutes before serving. Yield: 8 servings.

Individual Caramel Flans

¾ cup sugar, divided
½ cup skim milk
1 (12-ounce) can evaporated
   skimmed milk

¾ cup egg substitute
½ teaspoon almond extract
⅛ teaspoon salt
2 cups fresh strawberries, halved

Per serving:
Calories 173 (2% from fat)
Fat 0.3g (sat 0.1g;
   mono 0.1g; poly 0.1g)
Cholesterol 3mg
Sodium 170mg
Carbohydrate 35.0g
Fiber 0.8g
Protein 8.2g

Sprinkle ½ cup sugar in a small cast-iron skillet or other heavy skillet; place over medium heat. Cook, stirring constantly, until sugar melts and turns light golden. Pour caramelized syrup into six 6-ounce custard cups; set aside to cool. (Syrup may crack slightly as it cools.)

Combine skim milk and evaporated milk in a medium saucepan; cook over medium heat until bubbles form around edge of pan. (Do not boil.)

Combine remaining ¼ cup sugar, egg substitute, almond extract, and salt in a medium bowl. Gradually stir about 1 cup hot milk mixture into sugar mixture; add to remaining hot milk mixture, stirring constantly. Pour custard mixture evenly into prepared cups; cover each cup with aluminum foil.

Place cups in a shallow pan; add hot water to pan to depth of 1 inch. Bake at 325° for 40 minutes or until a knife inserted in center of custard comes out clean. Remove cups from water; uncover cups. Cool on a wire rack 30 minutes. Cover and chill at least 8 hours.

To serve, run a knife around edge of each cup to loosen custard. Invert cups onto individual serving plates. Arrange strawberry halves evenly around flans. Yield: 6 servings.

Vanilla Poached Pears

A glittery web of spun sugar envelops sweet, ripe
pears in this epitome of elegant desserts.

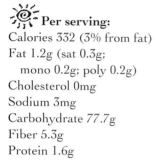 **Per serving:**
Calories 332 (3% from fat)
Fat 1.2g (sat 0.3g;
     mono 0.2g; poly 0.2g)
Cholesterol 0mg
Sodium 3mg
Carbohydrate 77.7g
Fiber 5.3g
Protein 1.6g

4 medium-size ripe Bosc pears
1 tablespoon lemon juice
4 cups water
3 tablespoons vanilla extract
2 tablespoons honey

½ cup sugar
3 drops hot water
Chocolate Sauce
Garnish: fresh mint sprigs

Peel pears, leaving stem ends intact. Core pears from bottoms, cutting to but not through stem ends. Cut a thin slice from base of each pear so that it will stand upright. Brush or rub pears with lemon juice.

Combine 4 cups water, vanilla, and honey in a large saucepan; bring to a boil. Place pears in pan. Cover, reduce heat, and simmer 10 minutes or until pears are just tender, turning occasionally. Remove pears from cooking liquid with a slotted spoon, discarding cooking liquid; cover pears, and chill.

Sprinkle sugar into a small cast-iron skillet or other heavy skillet; place over medium heat. Cook, stirring constantly, until sugar melts and turns light golden. Stir in drops of water. Remove from heat, and let stand 2 to 3 minutes or until caramelized syrup is slightly thickened.

Place a sheet of wax paper over work surface; position pears in an upright position on wax paper. Place skillet of caramelized syrup over low heat to keep syrup from hardening. Dip a fork into syrup; let excess drip back into skillet. When syrup begins to thread, move fork around a pear in a smooth, steady motion, working quickly. Repeat procedure until pear is covered in a blanket of spun sugar. Working quickly, repeat procedure with remaining caramelized syrup and pears. (Spun sugar will begin to dissolve in about 15 minutes.)

To serve, spoon 2 tablespoons Chocolate Sauce onto each serving plate; carefully place pears on sauce. Garnish, if desired, and serve immediately. Yield: 4 servings.

Chocolate Sauce

½ cup water
3 tablespoons sugar
2 tablespoons cocoa

1 teaspoon cornstarch
½ teaspoon vanilla extract

Combine all ingredients in a small saucepan; bring to a boil over medium heat, stirring constantly. Boil, stirring constantly, 1 minute. Cool. Yield: ½ cup.

Vanilla Poached Pear (facing page)

Layered Ambrosia

Enjoy this make-ahead dessert during the cold days
of winter when fresh citrus is at its juicy best.

3 cups fresh orange sections
1 cup fresh pink grapefruit
    sections
½ cup flaked coconut, divided

1 (8-ounce) can crushed pineapple
    in juice, undrained
3 tablespoons honey

Arrange half of orange sections in a medium glass bowl; top with grapefruit
sections, ¼ cup coconut, pineapple, and remaining orange sections. Drizzle
with honey, and sprinkle with remaining coconut. Cover and chill 8 hours.
Yield: 10 (½-cup) servings.

Per serving:
Calories 88 (17% from fat)
Fat 1.7g (sat 1.5g;
   mono 0.1g; poly 0.1g)
Cholesterol 0mg
Sodium 13mg
Carbohydrate 19.0g
Fiber 2.9g
Protein 0.9g

Fruit-Filled Chocolate Crêpes

Tender chocolate crêpes cuddle with juicy bits of fresh raspberries, orange, and kiwifruit in this refreshing dessert, pictured on page 71.

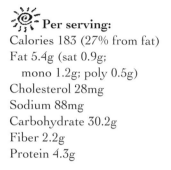

Per serving:
Calories 183 (27% from fat)
Fat 5.4g (sat 0.9g;
    mono 1.2g; poly 0.5g)
Cholesterol 28mg
Sodium 88mg
Carbohydrate 30.2g
Fiber 2.2g
Protein 4.3g

½ cup all-purpose flour
½ cup evaporated skimmed milk
1 tablespoon sugar
1 tablespoon cocoa
1 tablespoon reduced-calorie
    margarine, melted
1 egg
Vegetable cooking spray
½ cup fresh raspberries

½ cup fresh orange sections,
    coarsely chopped
2 medium kiwifruit, peeled and
    coarsely chopped
Chocolate Glaze
2 tablespoons sliced almonds,
    toasted
Garnish: fresh mint sprigs

Combine first 6 ingredients in container of an electric blender; cover and process at high until smooth. Chill batter at least 2 hours.

Coat bottom of a 6-inch crêpe pan or heavy skillet with cooking spray; place over medium heat until hot. Pour 2 tablespoons batter into pan; quickly tilt pan in all directions so batter covers bottom. Cook 1 minute or until crêpe can be shaken loose from pan. Turn crêpe; cook about 30 seconds. Place crêpe on a cloth towel to cool. Repeat procedure with remaining batter.

Stack crêpes between sheets of wax paper to prevent sticking. (At this point, crêpes may be placed in an airtight container and chilled up to 2 days or frozen up to 3 months.)

Place 1 crêpe on each individual dessert plate; spoon raspberries, chopped orange sections, and kiwifruit evenly onto half of each crêpe. Fold crêpes in half, and drizzle each with 1 tablespoon Chocolate Glaze. Sprinkle evenly with almonds. Garnish, if desired. Yield: 8 servings.

Chocolate Glaze

2 tablespoons reduced-calorie
    margarine
2 tablespoons cocoa

2 tablespoons water
1 cup sifted powdered sugar
½ teaspoon vanilla extract

Melt margarine in a small saucepan over low heat; add cocoa and water, stirring until smooth. Cook until mixture thickens, stirring often. (Do not boil.) Remove from heat; add powdered sugar and vanilla, stirring until smooth. Yield: ½ cup.

Pink Grapefruit and Tarragon Sorbet

Pink Grapefruit and Tarragon Sorbet

*Grapefruit and tarragon may sound like an unlikely pair, but
they're a match made in heaven in this exotic sorbet.*

1¾ cups sugar

1 cup water

2 (8-inch) sprigs fresh tarragon,
coarsely chopped

4 cups fresh pink grapefruit juice

Garnish: fresh tarragon sprigs

Per serving:
Calories 173 (0% from fat)
Fat 0.1g (sat 0.0g;
mono 0.0g; poly 0.0g)
Cholesterol 0mg
Sodium 1mg
Carbohydrate 43.9g
Fiber 0.0g
Protein 0.5g

Combine sugar and water in a medium saucepan; cook over medium heat,
stirring constantly, until sugar dissolves. Add chopped tarragon; bring to a
boil. Remove from heat; stir in grapefruit juice. Cover; chill at least 2 hours.

Pour mixture through a wire-mesh strainer into a 9-inch square pan, discarding tarragon. Cover and freeze until firm, stirring occasionally with a
wire whisk.

To serve, remove from freezer, and let stand 5 minutes. Scoop into dessert
dishes; garnish, if desired. Serve immediately. Yield: 10 (½-cup) servings.

INDEX

CREDITS

OXMOOR HOUSE WISHES TO THANK THE FOLLOWING MERCHANTS:

Almost Round/Americaware, Gardena, CA
Annieglass, Santa Cruz, CA
Augusta Glass Studio, Augusta, MO
BB's China & Glassware, Birmingham, AL
Bromberg and Co., Inc., Birmingham, AL
Carolyn Rice Art Pottery, Marietta, GA
Cassis & Co., New York, NY
Charlotte & Co., Birmingham, AL
Christine's, Birmingham, AL
Cyclamen Studio, Berkeley, CA
Daisy Arts, Venice, CA
Barbara Eigen, Jersey City, NJ
Fioriware, Zanesville, OH
Hotel Brazil, Birmingham, AL
Interiors Market, Birmingham, AL
The Loom Company, Aletha Soulé, New York, NY
Luna Garcia, Venice, CA
MacKenzie-Childs, Ltd., Aurora, NY
Mariposa, Gloucester, MA
Mesa International, Elkins, NH
Peggy Karr Glass, Cedar Knolls, NJ
Porta, Inc., Piscataway, NJ
Jill Rosenwald, Boston, MA
Sabre Flatware, Dallas, TX
Southern Settings, Birmingham, AL
Stonefish Pottery, Hartford, CT
Swid Powell, New York, NY
Table Matters, Birmingham, AL
Union Street Glass, Oakland, CA
Wigwam, Tetonia, ID

Metric Equivalents

The recipes that appear in this cookbook use the standard United States method for measuring liquid and dry or solid ingredients (teaspoons, tablespoons, and cups). The information in the following charts is provided to help cooks outside the U.S. successfully use these recipes. All equivalents are approximate.

Metric Equivalents for Different Types of Ingredients

A standard cup measure of a dry or solid ingredient will vary in weight depending on the type of ingredient. A standard cup of liquid is the same volume for any type of liquid. Use the following chart when converting standard cup measures to grams (weight) or milliliters (volume).

Standard Cup	Fine Powder (ex. flour)	Grain (ex. rice)	Granular (ex. sugar)	Liquid Solids (ex. butter)	Liquid (ex. milk)
1	140 g	150 g	190 g	200 g	240 ml
¾	105 g	113 g	143 g	150 g	180 ml
⅔	93 g	100 g	125 g	133 g	160 ml
½	70 g	75 g	95 g	100 g	120 ml
⅓	47 g	50 g	63 g	67 g	80 ml
¼	35 g	38 g	48 g	50 g	60 ml
⅛	18 g	19 g	24 g	25 g	30 ml

Useful Equivalents for Liquid Ingredients by Volume

¼ tsp				=	1 ml	
½ tsp				=	2 ml	
1 tsp				=	5 ml	
3 tsp	=	1 tbls	=	½ fl oz	=	15 ml
		2 tbls	= ⅛ cup =	1 fl oz	=	30 ml
		4 tbls	= ¼ cup =	2 fl oz	=	60 ml
		5⅓ tbls	= ⅓ cup =	3 fl oz	=	80 ml
		8 tbls	= ½ cup =	4 fl oz	=	120 ml
		10⅔ tbls	= ⅔ cup =	5 fl oz	=	160 ml
		12 tbls	= ¾ cup =	6 fl oz	=	180 ml
		16 tbls	= 1 cup =	8 fl oz	=	240 ml
		1 pt	= 2 cups =	16 fl oz	=	480 ml
		1 qt	= 4 cups =	32 fl oz	=	960 ml
				33 fl oz	=	1000 ml = 1 l

Useful Equivalents for Dry Ingredients by Weight

(To convert ounces to grams, multiply the number of ounces by 30)

1 oz	=	¹⁄₁₆ lb	=	30 g
4 oz	=	¼ lb	=	120 g
8 oz	=	½ lb	=	240 g
12 oz	=	¾ lb	=	360 g
16 oz	=	1 lb	=	480 g

Useful Equivalents for Length

(To convert inches to centimeters, multiply the number of inches by 2.5)

1 in			=	2.5 cm		
6 in	=	½ ft	=	15 cm		
12 in	=	1 ft	=	30 cm		
36 in	=	3 ft	= 1 yd =	90 cm		
40 in			=	100 cm	=	1 m

Useful Equivalents for Cooking/Oven Temperatures

	Fahrenheit	Celcius	Gas Mark
Freeze Water	32° F	0° C	
Room Temperature	68° F	20° C	
Boil Water	212° F	100° C	
Bake	325° F	160° C	3
	350° F	180° C	4
	375° F	190° C	5
	400° F	200° C	6
	425° F	220° C	7
	450° F	230° C	8
Broil			Grill